MORAL CULTURE OF INFANCY, AND KINDERGARTEN GUIDE

MORAL CULTURE OF INFANCY, AND KINDERGARTEN GUIDE

WITH MUSIC FOR THE PLAYS

HORACE MANN

&

ELIZABETH P. PEABODY

GYAN

Published by

Gyan Publishing House
5, Ansari Road
Daryaganj, New Delhi-110002
Phone: 011-47034999, 9811692060
E-mail: books@gyanbooks.com

Distribution Network
gyanbooks.com
India, USA, Canada, UK, Australia

ISBN: 978-93-7447-160-9 (PB)

First Published, 1863

2nd Impression 2026

Printed at: Gyan Press, Delhi.

MORAL CULTURE OF INFANCY, AND KINDERGARTEN GUIDE
Author: HORACE MANN AND ELIZABETH P. PEABODY

BCDGLOQRS

MORAL CULTURE OF INFANCY,

AND

KINDERGARTEN GUIDE,

With Music for the Plays.

BY

MRS. HORACE MANN,

AND

ELIZABETH P. PEABODY.

THIRD EDITION.

NEW YORK:

J. W. SCHEMERHORN & CO.

1870.

PREFACE.

It is in answer to a demand now become very general in this community, that I bring forward an American Kindergarten Guide. Kindergartens are springing up in all our cities. The French and English guides, and the Journals of *The New Education*, published in Germany and France, are expensive to import; and, besides, I think the selections I take from these sources, modified by my own views, make a book more suitable for American use than a foreign work can be.

I have persuaded my sister to give me her letters on the Moral Culture of Infancy, for an Appendix to my work, because moral culture is a twin object with physical culture in a Kindergarten; and the letters express the very spirit of Froebel, whose primary object was to give a moral and religious cast to the intelligence of healthy children.

The letters were written in the midst of the practical experiments they describe, in correspondence with Mrs. Lowell's "Letters on the Theory of Teaching," published in 1841. They could not be published at the same time, because they were so full of personal details, that the children spoken of would have been easily identified. After this lapse of time identification will not be easy. The circumstances of Mrs. Lowell's letters were imaginary, and they make a noble manual for governesses. But in both cases the letters were written for their authors' mutual understanding and improvement, with no view to publication; and are all the more genuine and valuable on that account.

I have reduced the price of my Guide, by leaving out the plates and directions for the use of Froebel's Gifts; because, without the Gifts, the directions are useless, and with them, superfluous. Two of these Gifts, intended for the nursery, have already been published in Boston, with the manuals for direction. And the other four, which are indispensable for the Kindergarten, will be published in one box with the manual of plates, as soon as the public shall demand it by specific orders. It would be an admirable investment of capital for some one to get up this; also a box of materials for pea-work, and one for weaving the little paper mats: in short, all the materials for the manipulations of the Kindergarten.

E. P. P.

15 Pinckney Street, Boston.

POSTSCRIPT.

I have been urged to publish these letters, written twenty years ago, as an appendix to a Kindergarten Guide, because the school herein described was a groping attempt at something of the same kind, and had left very pleasant memories in the hearts of the children referred to — now no longer children, but some of them men and women nobly and beautifully acting their parts on earth as parents; and others, — having died martyrs' deaths for human freedom in the desolating war that now ravages our beloved country, — angels in heaven.

If an inborn love of children and of school-keeping are qualifications for judging of the best means of educating them, I may claim to have known something of the theory and practice best adapted to that end. My object was to put them in possession of all their faculties. Many improvements in methods, and many facilities in means, have been added to the resources of teachers since these letters were written. Physical training is felt to be of the greatest importance, in preference to the ancient mode of shutting children up many hours in close rooms, and repressing all natural and joyous life. The principle is discovered of educating by *directing the activities.* Hence the Kindergarten.

M. M.

CONCORD, MASS., 1863.

CONTENTS.

CHAP.		PAGE
I.	Kindergarten — What is it?	9
II.	Rooms, etc.	25
III.	Music	28
IV.	Plays, Gymnastics, and Dancing	34
V.	Blocks, Sticks, and Peas	39
VI.	Manipulations	45
VII.	Moral and Religious Exercises	52
VIII.	Object Lessons	58
IX.	Geometry	65
X.	Arithmetic	72
XI.	Reading	75
XII.	Grammar and Languages	98
XIII.	Geography	103
XIV.	The Secret of Power	104

Moral Culture of Infancy 105

AMERICAN KINDERGARTEN.

CHAPTER I.

KINDERGARTEN — WHAT IS IT?*

WHAT is a Kindergarten? I will reply by negatives. It is not the old-fashioned infant-school. That was a narrow institution, comparatively; the object being (I do not speak of Pestalozzi's own, but that which we have had in this country and in England) to take the children of poor laborers, and keep them out of the fire and the streets, while their mothers went to their necessary labor. Very good things, indeed, in their way. Their principle of discipline was to circumvent the wills of children, in every way that would enable their teachers to keep them within bounds, and quiet. It was certainly better that they should learn to sing *by rote* the Creed and the "definitions" of scientific terms, and such like, than to learn the profanity and obscenity of the streets, which was the alternative. But no mother who wished for anything which might be called the *development* of her child would think of putting it into an infant-school, especially if she lived in the country, amid

> "the mighty sum
> Of things forever speaking,"

where any "old grey stone" would altogether surpass, as a stand-point, the bench of the highest class of an infant-school. In short, they did not state the problem of infant culture with any breadth, and accomplished nothing of general interest on the subject.

* First published in *Atlantic Monthly*, Nov. 1862.

Neither is the primary public school a Kindergarten, though it is but justice to the capabilities of that praiseworthy institution, so important in default of a better, to say that in one of them, at the North End of Boston, an enterprising and genial teacher has introduced one feature of Froebel's plan. She has actually given to each of her little children a box of playthings, wherewith to amuse itself according to its own sweet will, at all times when not under direct instruction, — necessarily, in her case, on condition of its being perfectly quiet; and this one thing makes this primary school the best one in Boston, both as respects the attainments of the scholars and their good behavior.

Kindergarten means a garden of children, and Froebel, the inventor of it, or rather, as he would prefer to express it, *the discoverer of the method of Nature*, meant to symbolize by the name the spirit and plan of treatment. How does the gardener treat his plants? He studies their individual natures, and puts them into such circumstances of soil and atmosphere as enable them to grow, flower, and bring forth fruit, — also to renew their manifestation year after year. He does not expect to succeed unless he learns all their wants, and the circumstances in which these wants will be supplied, and all their possibilities of beauty and use, and the means of giving them opportunity to be perfected. On the other hand, while he knows that they must not be forced against their individual natures, he does not leave them to grow wild, but prunes redundancies, removes destructive worms and bugs from their leaves and stems, and weeds from their vicinity, — carefully watching to learn what peculiar insects affect what particular plants, and how the former can be destroyed without injuring the vitality of the latter. After all the most careful gardener can do, he knows that the form of the plant is predetermined in the germ or seed, and that the inward tendency must concur with a multitude of influences, the most powerful and subtile of which is removed in place ninety-five millions of miles away.

In the Kindergarten, *children* are treated on an analogous plan. It presupposes gardeners of the mind, who are quite aware that they have as little power to override the characteristic individuality of a child, or to predetermine this characteristic, as the gardener of plants to say that a lily shall be a rose. But notwithstanding this limitation on one side, and the necessity for a concurrence of the Spirit on the other, — which is more independent of our modification than the remote sun, — yet they must feel responsible, after all, for the perfection of the development, in so far as removing every impediment, preserving every condition, and pruning every redundance.

This analogy of education to the gardener's art is so striking, both as regards what we can and what we cannot do, that Froebel has put every educator into a most suggestive Normal School, by the very word which he has given to his seminary, — Kindergarten.

If every school-teacher in the land had a garden of flowers and fruits to cultivate, it could hardly fail that he would learn to be wise in his vocation. For suitable preparation, the first, second, and third thing is, to

> "Come forth into the light of things,
> Let Nature be your teacher."

The "new education," as the French call it, begins with children in the mother's arms. Froebel had the nurses bring to his establishment, in Hamburg, children who could not talk, who were not more than three months old, and trained the nurses to work on his principles and by his methods. This will hardly be done in this country, at least at present; but to supply the place of such a class, a lady of Boston has prepared and published, under copyright, Froebel's First Gift, consisting of six soft balls of the three primary and the three secondary colors, which are sold in a box, with a little manual for mothers, in which the true principle and plan of tending babies, so as not to rasp their nerves, but to amuse without wearying them, is very happily suggested.

There is no mother or nurse who would not be assisted by this little manual essentially. As it says in the beginning, — "Tending babies is an art, and every art is founded on a science of observations; for love is not wisdom, but love must act *according to wisdom* in order to succeed. Mothers and nurses, however tender and kind-hearted, may, and oftenest do, weary and vex the nerves of children, in well-meant efforts to amuse them, and weary themselves the while. Froebel's exercises, founded on the observations of an intelligent sensibility, are intended to amuse without wearying, to educate without vexing."

Froebel's Second Gift for children, adapted to the age from one to two or three years, with another little book of directions, has also been published by the same lady, and is perhaps a still greater boon to every nursery; for this is the age when many a child's temper is ruined, and the inclination of the twig wrongly bent, through sheer *want of resource and idea,* on the part of nurses and mothers.

But it is to the next age — from three years old and upwards — that the Kindergarten becomes the desideratum, if not a necessity. The isolated home, made into a flower-vase by the application of the principles set forth in the Gifts above mentioned, may do for babies. But every mother and nurse knows how hard it is to meet the demands of a child too young to be taught to read, but whose opening intelligence and irrepressible bodily activity are so hard to be met by an adult, however genial and active. Children generally take the temper of their whole lives from this period of their existence. Then "the twig is bent," either towards that habit of self-defence which is an ever-renewing cause of selfishness, or to the sun of love-in-exercise, which is the exhaustless source of goodness and beauty.*

The indispensable thing now is a sufficient society of chil-

* If some large dealer would get up the other four Block Gifts in one box, with plates of direction taken from Rongé's Guide, there would be a large sale, for these blocks are indispensable (in the Kindergarten) to each child.

dren. It is only in the society of equals that the social instinct can be gratified, and come into equilibrium with the instinct of self-preservation. Self-love, and love of others, are equally natural; and before reason is developed, and the proper spiritual life begins, sweet and beautiful childhood may bloom out and imparadise our mortal life. Let us only give the social instinct of children its fair chance. For this purpose, a few will not do. The children of one family are not enough, and do not come along fast enough. A large company should be gathered out of many families. It will be found that the little things are at once taken out of themselves, and become interested in each other. In the variety, affinities develop themselves very prettily, and the rough points of rampant individualities wear off. We have seen a highly-gifted child, who, at home, was — to use a vulgar, but expressive word — pesky and odious, with the exacting demands of a powerful, but untrained mind and heart, become "sweet as roses" spontaneously, amidst the rebound of a large, well-ordered, and carefully watched child-society. Anxious mothers have brought us children, with a thousand deprecations and explanations of their characters, as if they thought we were going to find them little monsters, which their motherly hearts were persuaded they were not, though they behaved like little sanchos at home, — and, behold, they were as harmonious, from the very beginning, as if they had undergone the subduing influence of a lifetime. We are quite sure that children begin with loving others quite as intensely as they love themselves, — forgetting themselves in their love of others, — if they only have as fair a chance of being benevolent and self-sacrificing as of being selfish. Sympathy is as much a natural instinct as self-love, and no more or less innocent, in a moral point of view. Either principle alone makes an ugly and depraved form of natural character. Balanced, they give the element of happiness, and the conditions of spiritual goodness and truth, — making children fit temples for the Holy Ghost to dwell in.

A Kindergarten, then, is children in society, — a commonwealth or republic of children, — whose laws are all part and parcel of the Higher Law alone. It may be contrasted, in every particular, with the old-fashioned school, which is an absolute monarchy, where the children are subjected to a lower expediency, having for its prime end quietness, or such order as has "reigned in Warsaw" since 1831.

But let us not be misunderstood. We are not of those who think that children, in any condition whatever, will inevitably develop into beauty and goodness. Human nature tends to revolve in a vicious circle, around the idiosyncrasy; and children must have over them, in the person of a wise and careful teacher, a power which shall deal with them as God deals with the mature, presenting the claims of sympathy and truth whenever they presumptuously or unconsciously fall into selfishness. We have the best conditions of moral culture in a company large enough for the exacting disposition of the solitary child to be balanced by the claims made by others on the common stock of enjoyment, — there being a reasonable oversight of older persons, wide-awake to anticipate, prevent, and adjust the rival pretensions which must always arise where there are finite beings with infinite desires, while Reason, whose proper object is God, is yet undeveloped.

Let the teacher always take for granted that the law of love is quick within, whatever are appearances, and the better self will generally respond. In proportion as the child is young and unsophisticated, will be the certainty of the response to a teacher of simple faith:

> "There are who ask not if thine eye
> Be on them, — who, in love and truth,
> Where no misgiving is, rely
> Upon the genial sense of youth.
>
> "And blest are they who in the main
> This faith even now do entertain,
> Live in the spirit of this creed,
> Yet find another strength, according to their need."

Such are the natural Kindergartners, who prevent disorder by employing and entertaining children, so that they are kept in an accommodating and loving mood by never being thrown on self-defence, — and when selfishness is aroused, who check it by an appeal to sympathy, or Conscience, which is the presentiment of Reason, a fore-feeling of moral order, for whose culture material order is indispensable.

But order must be kept by the child, not only unconsciously, but intentionally. Order is the child of reason, and in turn cultivates the intellectual principle. To bring out order on the physical plane, the Kindergarten makes it a serious purpose to organize *romping*, and set it to music, which cultivates the physical nature also. Romping is the ecstasy of the body, and we shall find that in proportion as children tend to be violent they are vigorous in body. There is always morbid weakness of some kind where there is no instinct for hard play; and it begins to be the common sense that energetic physical activity must not be repressed, but favored. Some plan of play prevents the little creatures from hurting each other, and fancy naturally furnishes the plan, — the mind unfolding itself in fancies, which are easily quickened and led in harmless directions by an adult of any resource. Those who have not imagination themselves must seek the aid of the Kindergarten guides, where will be found arranged to music the labors of the peasant, and cooper, and sawyer, the wind-mill, the water-mill, the weather-vane, the clock, the pigeon-house, the hares, the bees, and the cuckoo. Children delight to personate animals, and a fine genius could not better employ itself than in inventing a great many more plays, setting them to rhythmical words, describing what is to be done. Every variety of bodily exercise might be made and kept within the bounds of order and beauty by plays involving the motions of different animals and machines of industry. Kindergarten plays are easy intellectual exercises; for to do anything whatever with a thought beforehand, develops the mind or quickens the intelligence; and thought of this kind does not tax intellect, or check physical development, which last must never be sacrificed in the process of education.

There are enough instances of marvellous acquisition in infancy to show that imbibing with the mind is as natural as with the body, if suitable beverage is put to the lips; but in most cases the mind's power is balanced by instincts of body, which should have priority, if they cannot certainly be in full harmony. The mind can afford to wait for the maturing of the body, for it survives the body; while the body cannot afford to wait for the mind, but is irretrievably stunted, if the nervous energy is not free to stimulate its special organs, at least equally with those of the mind.

It is not, however, the intention to sacrifice the culture of either mind or body, but to harmonize them. They can and ought to grow together. They mutually help each other.

Dr. Dio Lewis's "Free Exercises" are suitable to the Kindergarten, and may be taken in short lessons of a quarter of an hour, or even of ten minutes. Children are fond of precision also, and it will be found that they like the teaching best, when they are made to do the exercises exactly right, and in perfect time to the music.

But the regular gymnastics and the romping plays must be alternated with quiet employments, of course, but still active. They will sing at their plays by rote; and also should be taught other songs by rote. But there can be introduced a regular drill on the scale, which should never last more than ten minutes at a time. This, if well managed, will cultivate their ears and voices, so that in the course of a year they will become very expert in telling any note struck, if not in striking it. The ear is cultivated sooner than the voice, and they may be taught to name the octave as 1, 2, 3, 4, 5, 6, 7, 8, while their imaginations are impressed by drawing a ladder of eight rounds on the blackboard, to signify that the voice rises by regular gradation. This will fix their attention, and their interest will not flag, if the teacher has any tact.

Slates and pencils are indispensable in a Kindergarten from the first. One side of a slate can be ruled with a sharp point in small squares, and if their fancy is interested by telling them to make a fish-net, they will carefully make their pencils follow these lines, — which makes a first exercise in drawing. Their little fingers are so unmanageable that at first they will not be able to make straight lines even with this help. For variety, little patterns can be given them, drawn on the blackboard, (or on paper similarly ruled,) of picture-frames and patterns for carpets. When they can make squares well, they can be shown how to cross them with diagonals, and make circles inside of the squares, and outside of them, and encouraged to draw on the other side of the slate from their own fancy, or from objects. Entire sympathy and no destructive criticism should meet every effort. Self-confidence is the first requisite for success. If they think they have had success, it is indispensable that it should be echoed from without. Of course there will be poor perspective; even Schmidt's method of perspective cannot be introduced to very young children. A natural talent for perspective sometimes shows itself, which by-and-by can be perfected by Schmidt's method.*

But little children will not draw long at a time. Nice manipulation, which is important, can be taught, and the eye for form cultivated, by drawing for them birds and letting them prick the lines. It will enchant them to have something pretty to carry home now and then. Perforated board can also be used to teach them the use of a needle and thread. They will like to make the outlines of ships and steamboats, birds, &c., which can be drawn for them with a lead pencil on the board by the teachers. Weaving strips of colored card-board into papers cut for them is another enchanting amusement, and can be made subservient to teaching them the harmonies of colors. In the latter part of the season, when they have an accumulation of pricked birds, or have

* See *Common School Journal* for 1842–3.

learned to draw them, they can be allowed colors to paint them in a rough manner. It is, perhaps, worth while to say, that, in teaching children to draw on their slates, it is better for the teacher to draw at the moment on the blackboard than to give them patterns of birds, utensils, etc., because then the children will see how to begin and proceed, and are not discouraged by the mechanical perfection of their model.

Drawing ought always rather to precede reading and writing, as the minute appreciation of forms is the proper preparation for these. But reading and writing may come into Kindergarten exercises at once, if reading is taught by the phonic method, (which saves all perplexity to the child's brain,) and accompanied by printing on the slate. It then alternates with other things, as one of the amusements. We will describe how we have seen it taught. The class sat before a blackboard, with slates and pencils. The teacher said,—"Now let us make all the sounds that we can with the lips: First, put the lips gently together and sound m," (not *em*,) — which they all did. Then she said, — "Now let us draw it on the blackboard, — three short straight marks by the side of each other, and join them on the top, — that is m. What is it?" They sounded m, and made three marks and joined them on the top, with more or less success. The teacher said, — "Now put your lips close together and say p." (This is mute and to be whispered.) They all imitated the motion made. She said, — "Now let us write it; one straight mark, then the upper lip puffed out at the top." M and p, to be written and distinguished, are perhaps enough for one lesson, which should not reach half an hour in length. At the next lesson these were repeated again. Then the teacher said, — "Now put your lips together and make the same motion as you did to say p; but make a little more sound, and it will be b" (which is sonorous). "You must write it differently from p; — you must make a short mark and put the *under* lip on." "Now put your teeth on your under lip and say f." (She gave the power.) "You must write it by making a short straight mark make a bow, and then cross it with a little mark across the middle." "Now fix your lips in the same manner and sound a little, and you will make v. Write it by making two little marks meet at the bottom."

This last letter was made a separate lesson of, and the other lessons were reviewed. The teacher then said,—"Now you have learned some letters,—all the lip-letters,"—making them over, and asking what each was. She afterwards added w,—giving its power and form, and put it with the lip-letters. At the next lesson they were told to make the letters with their lips, and she wrote them down on the board, and then said,—"Now we will make some tooth-letters. Put your teeth together and say t." (She gave the power, and showed them how to write it.) "Now put your teeth together and make a sound and it will be d." "That is written just like b, only we put the lip behind." "Now put your teeth together and hiss, and then make this little crooked snake (s). Then fix your teeth in the same manner and buzz like a bee. You write z pointed this way." "Now put your teeth together and say j, written with a dot." At the next lesson the throat-letters were given; first the hard guttural was sounded, and they were told three ways to write it, c, k, q, distinguished as *round*, *high*, and *with a tail*. C was not sounded *see*, but c and k and q alike (*ik*). Another lesson gave them the soft guttural g, but did not sound it *jee;* and the aspirate h, but did not call it *aitch*.

Another lesson gave the vowels, (or voice-letters, as she called them,) and it was made lively by her writing afterwards all of them in one word, *mieaou*, and calling it the cat's song. It took from a week to ten days to teach these letters, one lesson a day of about twenty minutes. Then came words: mamma, papa, puss, pussy, etc. The vowels always sounded as in Italian, and i and y were distinguished as *with a dot* and *with a tail*.

At first only one word was the lesson, and the letters were reviewed in their divisions of lip-letters, throat-letters, tooth-letters, voice-letters. The latter were sounded the Italian way, as in the words *a*rm, *e*gg, *i*nk, *o*ak, and Per*u*. This teacher had Miss Peabody's "First Nursery Reading-Book," and when she had taught the class to make all the words on the first page of it, she gave each of the children the book, and told them to find first one word and then another. It was a great pleasure to them to be told that now they could read. They were encouraged to copy the words out of the book upon their slates.

The "First Nursery Reading-Book" has in it *no* words that have exceptions in their spelling to the sounds given to the children as the powers of the letters. Nor has it any diphthong or combinations of letters, such as oi, ou, ch, sh, th. After they could read it at sight, they were told that all words were not so regular, and their attention was called to the initial sounds of thin, shin, and chin, and to the proper diphthongs, ou, oi, and au, and they wrote words considering these as additional characters. Then "Mother Goose," was put into their hands, and they were made to read by rote the songs they already knew by heart, and to copy them. It was a great entertainment to find the *queer* words, and these were made the nucleus of groups of similar words which were written on the blackboard and copied on their slates.

We have thought it worth while to give in detail this method of teaching to read, because it is the most entertaining to children to be taught so, and because many successful instances of the pursuit of this plan have come under our observation; and one advantage of it has been, that the children so taught, though never going through the common spelling-lessons, have uniformly exhibited a rare exactness in orthography.

In going through this process, the children learn to print very nicely, and generally can do so sooner than they can read. It is a small matter afterwards to teach them to turn the print into script. They should be taught to write with the lead pencil before the pen, whose use need not come into the Kindergarten.

But we must not omit one of the most important exercises for children in the Kindergarten, — that of block-building. Froebel has four Gifts of blocks. Rongé's "Kindergarten Guide" has pages of royal octavo filled with engraved forms, that can be made by variously laying eight little cubes, and sixteen little planes two inches long, one inch broad, and one-half an inch thick. Chairs, tables, stables, sofas, garden-seats, and innumerable forms of symmetry, make an immense resource for children, who also should be led to invent other forms and imitate other objects. So quick are the fancies of children, that the blocks will serve also as symbols of everything in Nature and imagination. We have seen an ingenious teacher assemble a class of children around her large table, to each of whom she had given the blocks. The first thing was to count them, a great process of arithmetic to most of them. Then she made something and explained it. It was perhaps a light-house, — and some blocks would represent rocks near it to be avoided, and ships sailing in the ocean; or perhaps it was a hen-coop, with chickens inside, and a fox prowling about outside, and a boy who was going to catch the fox and save the fowls. Then she told each child to make something, and when it was done hold up a hand. The first one she asked to explain, and then went round the class. If one began to speak before another had ended, she would hold up her finger and say, — "It is not your turn." In the course of the winter, she taught, over these blocks, a great deal about the habits of animals. She studied natural history in order to be perfectly accurate in her symbolic representation of the habitation of each animal, and their enemies were also represented by blocks. The children imitated these; and when they drew upon their imaginations for facts, and made fantastic creations, she would say, — "Those, I think, were fairy hens" (or whatever); for it was her principle to accept everything, and thus tempt out their invention. The great value of this exercise is to get them into the habit of representing something they have thought by an outward symbol. The explanations they are always eager to give, teach them to express themselves in words. Full scope is given to invention, whether in the direction of possibilities or of the impossibilities in which children's imaginations revel, — in either case the child being trained to the habit of embodiment of its thought.

Froebel thought it very desirable to have a garden where the children could cultivate flowers. He had one which he divided into lots for the several children, reserving a portion for his own share in which they could assist him. He thought it the happiest mode of calling their attention to the invisible God, whose power must be waited upon, after the conditions for growth are carefully arranged according to *laws* which they must observe. Where a garden is impossible, a flower-pot with a plant in it, for each child to take care of, would do very well.

But the best way to cultivate a sense of the presence of God is to draw the attention to the conscience, which is very active in children, and which seems to them (as we all can testify from our own remembrance) another than themselves, and yet themselves. We have heard a person say, that in her childhood she was puzzled to know which was herself, the voice of her inclination or of her conscience, for they were palpably two; and what a joyous thing it was when she was first convinced that one was the Spirit of God, whom unlucky teaching had previously embodied in a form of terror on a distant judgment-seat. Children are consecrated as soon as they get the spiritual idea, and it may be so presented that it shall make them happy as well as true. But the adult who enters into such conversation with a child must be careful not to shock and profane, instead of nurturing the soul. It is possible to avoid both discouraging and flattering views, and to give the most tender and elevating associations.

But children require not only an alternation of physical and mental amusements, but some instruction to be passively received. They delight in stories, and a wise teacher can make this subservient to the highest uses by reading beautiful creations of the imagination. Not only such household-stories as "Sanford and Merton," Mrs. Farrar's "Robinson Crusoe," and Salzmann's "Elements of Morality," but symbolization like the heroes of Asgard, the legends of the Middle Ages, classic and chivalric tales, the legend of Saint George, and "Pilgrim's Progress," can in the mouth of a skilful reader be made subservient to moral culture. The reading sessions should not exceed ten or fifteen minutes.

Anything of the nature of scientific teaching should be done by presenting *objects* for examination and investigation.* Flowers and insects, shells, etc., are easily handled. The observations should be drawn out of the children, not made to them, except as corrections of their mistakes. Experiments with the prism, and in crystallization and transformation, are useful and desirable to awaken taste for the sciences of Nature. In short, the Kindergarten should give the beginnings of everything. "What is well begun is half done."

We must say a word about the locality and circumstances of a Kindergarten. There is published in Lausanne, France, a newspaper devoted to the interests of this mode of education, in whose early numbers is described a Kindergarten; which seems to be of the nature of a boarding-school; at least, the children are there all day. Each child has a garden, and there is one besides where they work in common. There are accommodations for keeping animals, and miniature tools to do mechanical labor of various kinds. In short, it is a child's world. But in this country, especially in New England, parents would not consent to be so much separated from their children, and a few hours of Kindergarten in the

* Calkin's *Object Lessons* will give hints.

early part of the day will serve an excellent purpose,— using up the effervescent activity of children, who may healthily be left to themselves the rest of the time, to play or rest, comparatively unwatched.

Two rooms are indispensable, if there is any variety of age. It is desirable that one should be sequestrated to the quiet employments. A pianoforte is desirable, to lead the singing, and accompany the plays, gymnastics, frequent marchings, and dancing, when that is taught, — which it should be. But a hand-organ which plays fourteen tunes will help to supply the want of a piano, and a guitar in the hands of a ready teacher will do better than nothing.

Sometimes a genial mother and daughters might have a Kindergarten, and devote themselves and the house to it, especially if they live in one of our beautiful country-towns or cities. The habit, in the city of New York, of sending children to school in an omnibus, hired to go round the city and pick them up, suggests the possibility of a Kindergarten in one of those beautiful residences up in town, where there is a garden before or behind the house. It is impossible to keep Kindergarten *by the way*. It must be the main business of those who undertake it; for it is necessary that every individual child should be borne, as it were, on the heart of the *gardeners*, in order that it be *inspired* with order, truth, and goodness. To develop a child from within outwards, we must plunge ourselves into its peculiarity of imagination and feeling. No one person could possibly endure such absorption of life in labor unrelieved, and consequently two or three should unite in the undertaking in order to be able to relieve each other from the enormous strain on life. The compensations are, however, great. The charm of the various individuality, and of the refreshing presence of conscience yet unprofaned, is greater than can be found elsewhere in this work-day world. Those were not idle words which came from the lips of Wisdom Incarnate: — "Their angels do always behold the face of my Father:" "Of such is the kingdom of heaven."

CHAPTER II.

ROOMS, ETC.

I HAVE made an article, which I published in the "Atlantic Monthly" of November, 1862, my first chapter, because I cannot, in any better way, answer the general question, — What is a Kindergarten? I will now proceed to make a Guide for the conduct of a Kindergarten; in which I shall freely make use of what Madame Rongé has said in her "English Kindergarten," and Madame Marienholtz in her "Jardin des Enfans;" but I shall not confine myself to them, for an American Kindergarten necessarily has its peculiarities.

In the first place, we must think of the accommodations. These are not to be in the open air, as has been supposed by many, through misapprehension of the use of the word Kindergarten. But it is desirable that there should be a good play-ground attached to the rooms; and Froebel thought it of very important religious influence that every child should have earth to cultivate, if it were only a foot square.

Two rooms are indispensable, and if possible there should be three, all of good size, with good light and air: one room for music and plays, gymnastics, dancing, &c.; another for the quieter mechanical employments, — pricking, weaving, sewing, moulding, folding, paper-cutting, sticklaying, and block-building; and still another for drawing, writing, object-teaching, and learning to read. It is desirable that every child should have a box, if not a little desk, in order to learn to keep things in order. When this cannot be done, the teachers must so arrange matters, as to have everything ready for every change; that no time may be lost and no confusion arise. In my own Kindergarten, I arrange beforehand the chairs in the play-room in a solid square, into which the children march at the commencement of the exercises. Sitting in them, they sing their morning prayer or hymn, hear the reading, and take a singing lesson on the scale. Then they rise, and, taking up their chairs, march into the other room for their reading lessons, which are always in two classes, sometimes in three. They bring their chairs back again for luncheon, and then take them out for another lesson; for in this room they have gymnastics, dancing, and the play, and need a clear space for all. They come back with their chairs, at the close of the exercises, to sing songs together before they disperse. Two of my rooms are carpeted. The other is smooth-floored for dancing, playing, and gymnastics. And, for the convenience of the gymnastics, it is well to paint, at convenient distances, *little feet in the first position*, as Dr. Dio Lewis has done in his gymnastic hall.

When Kindergarten accommodations can be built expressly, I would suggest that there should be a house with glass walls and partitions, at least above the wainscoting; and that the wainscoting should be rather high and painted black, so that every child might have a piece of the blackboard; for it is easier for a child to draw with a chalk on a blackboard than with a slate and pencil.

A house of glass, on the plan of the crystal palace, would be no more expensive than if built of brick. It would secure the light and sunshine, and make it easy for the superintendent to overlook the whole. It should be equably warmed throughout. My own Kindergarten is not in a glass house, but is the lower floor of a house which has three rooms, with a hall between two of the rooms; a large china closet which I use for the children's dressing, as well as to store many things; and beyond the third room, a bathing room, with every convenience. Rooms, hall, closet, and bathing room have all an east-south aspect, and are amply lighted. The room between the china closet and bathing room is longer than it is wide, and has blackboard painted on three sides of it, so that each child has a piece of blackboard.

It is possible to keep a Kindergarten in two rooms, but not possible to keep it in one, if it is of any desirable size, or there is any variety of age in the children. A large playground and some garden is desirable. I am so fortunate as to have these in my house in Boston.

There must be a musical instrument in every Kindergarten, of course. The only books which the children use are those in which they learn to read. Everything else must be taught by symbols, objects, and pictures, explained conversationally.

One of the rooms it would be well to provide with *flat* box-desks, in which can be kept all the materials which each child uses, — slates and pencils, blocks, sticks, weaving and sewing materials, — and the children should be required to keep these in order.

In my own Kindergarten I provide all the materials for their work and instruction, thus securing uniformity; and it is better to do so always, and to charge a price covering the expense. It should be understood, from the first, that Kindergarten education is not cheap.

As a Kindergarten requires several persons to keep it properly, a genial family, consisting of a mother and daughters, of various accomplishments, might devote their whole house to it, preparing for the writing and drawing one large room with blackboards all round, whose area could be used for the playing, gymnastics, and dancing.

When this new culture shall be appreciated for its whole worth, it will not be deemed extravagant for a whole family thus to devote their house, as well as their time, to make a Kindergarten the temporary home of a large company of children.

CHAPTER III.

MUSIC.

THE first requisite to the Kindergarten is Music. The voice of melody commands the will of the child, or rather disarms the caprice, which is the principle of disorder. Two hymns are given in this Guide with which to commence school, — one being the Lord's Prayer, set to cheerful music.

But there should be regular scale singing, and if conducted by a teacher of tact, a ten minutes lesson may be given every day, and the interest be kept undiminished. The first lesson should be preceded by the teacher's drawing on the blackboard a ladder of eight steps, and then saying to the pupils, "Now listen to my voice, and see how it goes up these steps." She then sings the eight notes very clearly, pointing to each step of the ladder; and runs her voice, with equal distinctness, down the descending scale. The children can then be asked to accompany the teacher in going up and down the ladder, singing the numbers 1, 2, 3, 4, 5, 6, 7, 8, instead of *do, re, mi.* There will doubtless be enough discords to be palpable to all ears, and these can be spoken of by the teacher, and a proposition made that every one who thinks he can go up and down the ladder alone, shall hold up a hand. Some may be able to do so, but a majority will fail. Some will not try at all.

The teacher can then say, "Now I am going to teach you all to do it, — one step at a time. Let us all sing *one.*" The piano is struck, and teacher and pupils all sing *one.* "Now let us go up a step, — one, two." Let this be repeated several times. Then stop, and say, "Now I am going to strike one of these notes and see if you know it." Strike two, and ask, "What is that, 1 or 2?" There may be difference of opinion; in which case, ask all to "hold up their hands who think it is 2, and then all who think it is 1." Tell which is right, and say, "Now let us all sing 2." Then say, "Now let us go down that step,—2, 1; and now up again,—1, 2; now all hold up their hands who can sing 1, 2, 1?" Select one after another to sing it alone with the piano, and after each has tried, let all sing with the teacher 1, 2, 1, before another is asked to sing it. Then let all sing 1, 1, 1; 2, 2, 2; 1, 1, 1. Go on in this way till all the eight notes are learned. They will be able to tell these notes, when struck upon the piano, much sooner than they will be able to strike them with their voices. And other exercises, every day calling upon them to name notes struck,—at first one note, afterwards combinations of notes.

The following exercises were given in my Kindergarten in one year, which resulted in nearly all the children being able to sing them alone, and tell any notes struck.

1st.—1 2 1; 1 1, 2 2, 1 1; 1 1 1 1, 2 2 2 2, 1 1 1 1, 2 1 2, &c.

2d.—1 2 3, 3 2 1; 1 3 3 1, 1 2 1, 2 3 2, 3 2 1.

3d.—1 2 3 4 5, 5 4 3 2 1. 1 3 5, 5 3 1, 1 5 5 1.

4th.—1 2 3 4 5 6; 6 5 4 3 2 1; 1 6, 6 1; 1 3 5 6.

5th.—1 2 3 4 5 6 7, 7 6 5 4 3 2 1; 1 3 5 8, 8 5 3 1.

6th.—1 2 3 4 5 6 7 8, 8 7 5 6 4 3 2 1; 1 3 5 8.

This exercise can be varied by repeating each note one two, three, or four times.

7th.—1 1 2, 2 2 3, 3 3 4, 4 4 5, 5 5 6, 7 7 8, 8 7 6 5 4 3 2 1.

8th.—1 1 2, 3 3 4, 5 5 6, 7 7 8; 8 7 6 5 4 3 2 1.

9th.—1 2, 1 2 1; 2 3, 2 3 2; 3 4, 3 4 3; 4 5, 4 5 6; 5 6, 5 6 7; 6 7, 6 7 8; 8, 7, 6, 5, 4, 3, 2, 1.

10th.—1 1, 2 2, 1; 2 2, 3 3, 2; 3 3, 4 4, 3; 4 4, 5 5, 4; &c.

11th.—1 3; 2 4; 3 5; 4 6; 5 7; 6 8; 8, 6; 7, 5; 6, 4; 5, 3; 4, 2; 3, 1.

12th.—1 3 5 8, 8 5 3 1; 1 4 6 8, 8 6 4 1; 1 8 8 1.

13th.—1 1, 3 3; 5 5, 8 8; 8 8, 7 7, 6 6, 5 5, 4 4, 3 3, 2 2, 1 1.

14th.—1 2 3 2 1; 2 3 4 3 2; 3 4 5 4 3; 4 5 6 5 4; 5 6 7 6 5; 6 7 8 7 6; 7 8 7 6 5 4 3 2 1.

15th.—1 2 1 2 3 3; 2 3 2 3 4 4; 3 4 3 4 5 5; 4 5 4 5 6 6; 5 6 5 6 7 7; 6 7 6 7 8 8; 8 8 8 8; 7 7 7 7; 6 6 6 6; 5 5 5 5; 4 4 4 4; 3 3 3 3; 2 2 2 2; 1 1 1 1; 1 8; 8 1.

Besides these ten minutes on the scale, (which should not occur next to singing the hymn, but after some other exercise has intervened,) it is an excellent plan to let the Kindergarten close with singing songs by rote. The words should be simple, such as "The Cat and the Sparrow," and other pretty melodies to be found in the Pestalozzian Singing Book and the many compilations prepared for children. For it is well for the child not to go out of the natural octave, and to have the words of songs adapted to the childish capacity. Besides this singing, the piano-forte should be used to play marches, as the children go from one room to another to their different exercises. "Order is Heaven's first law," and music is the heavenly voice of order, which disposes to gentleness and regularity of motion. As all the exercises change every quarter of an hour at least, this brings the marching to music as often; and it will last one or two minutes, sometimes longer. The children get accustomed to rise at the sound of the piano, and it will be easy to make them silent during the music, especially if it is hinted to them that *soldiers* always march in silence. Besides this, the piano is necessary for the gymnastics, and for the fanciful plays, which are always to be accompanied by descriptive songs.

A few songs and plays are given in this Guide, which, if taken in turn, will recur not oftener than once in ten days. We subjoin a description of the plays.

I will finish this chapter by a translation from a notice of "Enseignement Musical, d'aprés Froebel, par Fred. Stern, prix, 2 francs : En vente à Bruxelles, rue de Vienne, 16, et à Paris, rue Fossés St. Victor, 35." "A man to be complete, should be master of linear and musical expression. Most of our education aims only to give him lingual expression; and drawing and music are considered accomplishments merely ! The divine art which enables us to reproduce the human figure illuminated with the expression of the spirit, a mere accomplishment ! * Music, the melodious expression of our most intimate thoughts, the colored reflection of the heart, — a mere accomplishment !

"Life is sad, monotonous, earthy, without the arts. If a woman of the middle and higher classes especially, does not daily realize the higher life by knowledge of truth and love of beauty, what shall save her from the frivolity and *ennui* that gnaws away the heart, tarnishes the soul, and brings misfortune to the fireside? Every woman should be an artist, and make artists of her children, if she would do a woman's whole duty. Especially should the mother teach her children to *improvise* music, which can be done by pursuing this method.

"He commences by the study of the three sounds constituting the major triad, and, as in the model gamut, *or gamut of do*, there are three similar triads, three perfect major chords, do-mi-sol, fa-la-do, and sol-si-re, we begin naturally with the central chord, do-mi-sol, which we name the master chord; for, in the model gamut of do, it is around this, as around a centre, that the two other triads balance themselves, the lower fifth, fal-la-do, and the higher fifth, sol-si-re. We can show the unity of plan between these three established notes, in all the possible changes. We thus introduce a fine variety

* There is no excuse for its being so considered in Boston, now that Dr. Rimmer, the remarkable sculptor of the Falling Gladiator, has founded the true method of teaching to draw the human figure. It is indeed a method which it is not probable any person of less profound knowledge of the human figure than himself, (a practical surgeon as well as artist,) together with genius less bold and original, can conduct as he does; unless he shall train such teachers.

into the exercises, which permits the repetition of the same sounds and intervals, without causing fatigue or weariness to the child.

"Scarcely have our pupils learned to sing or to repeat alone, at will, the three sounds do-mi-sol, when we have them mark them with pencils on the staff (key of sol) ; only as in the unity of tone there are yet the two other perfect chords, fa-la-do and sol-si-re, we let them write the three notes of the central chord with a red pencil, and reserve the three sounds of the chord on the left, (the lower or subdominant,) to be written with a yellow pencil, and the chord on the right, (higher or dominant,) with a blue pencil. On the other hand, for the appellative chords (dissonant,) made by the combination of the chord sol-si-re, with one, two, and even three notes of the chord fa-la-do, we use green pencils (mixture of blue and yellow). For we would keep the theory in mind by visible signs, which act most powerfully upon the minds of children.

"Then we pass to perfect minor chords, and terminate this first branch of our method by the study of the gamut.

"Our pupil knows as yet only a single tone, — the tone of *do*, which we designate by the name of model tone ; — but all musicians are aware that to know well one tone, is to know them all, since they are all calculated on the model tone with which we began. The second part of our method will treat of the other tones, but it will prove no serious difficulty to our pupil.

"We have carefully avoided scientific terms, though doubtless, by a learned terminology, we should have struck superficial minds more. But we address ourselves to the serious, who know that it is better to know a thing in itself, (in what constitutes it essentially,) without knowing its technology, than to know obscure terms and be ignorant of the thing.

"Later, we shall initiate our pupil into the language generally adopted by all treatises on harmony. We wish that one day he may be a distinguished harmonist, knowing musical grammar at the foundation. It is strange that the study of grammar, so vigorously recommended for all other languages, is so entirely neglected in respect to musical language. The study of harmony seems to be reserved exclusively to artists; and even among them, only the few who are occupied with composing devote themselves to it with any profoundness. It is to this culpable negligence that we must attribute the difficulties of musical education. Where is the intelligent musician who would dare to deny the happy results inseparable from the most profound study of music? The scholar would necessarily have to give much less time to know the art in the best manner, which is now accessible only to remarkable persons of strong will. The grammatical study of music should begin at the same time as all other studies, and soon music would become the language of all, instead of being reserved exclusively to the privileged.

"Doubtless great reforms will be necessary to arrive at this result, and the spirit of routine which unhappily reigns everywhere will render such reforms difficult.

"However, we found great hopes on the inevitable development of the method of Froebel, for the principles he lays down are of general application." . . . . .

I am myself so profoundly impressed with the importance of little children's beginning music in this manner, that, having found a teacher who is capable of it, I intend, another year, to have extra hours for those who will commence instrumental music, in my own Kindergarten; so that each child can have a lesson *every day*, and only play under the eye of the teacher until quite expert.

CHAPTER IV.

PLAYS, GYMNASTICS, AND DANCING.

In playing The Pigeon-house, the teacher, who should always play with the children, takes three quarters of the number, and forms them into a circle, while the other quarter remains in the middle, to represent the pigeons.

The circle is the pigeon-house, and sings the song, beginning with the words:

"We open the pigeon-house again,"

while, standing still, they all hold up their joined hands, so as to let all the pigeons out at the word "open;" and, as the circle goes round singing,

"And let all the happy flutterers free,
They fly o'er the fields and grassy plain,
Delighted with glorious liberty,"

the pigeons run round, waving their hands up and down to imitate flying. At the word "return," in the line

"And when they return from their joyous flight,"

the joined hands of those in circle are lifted up again, and the pigeons go in. Then the pigeon-house closes round them, bowing their heads, and singing,

"We shut up the house and bid them good-night,"

which is repeated while the circle swings off and again comes together bowing.

The play can be done over until all in turn have been pigeons.

In playing Hare in the Hollow, a fourth of the children sit in the middle, on their hands and feet, while the rest, in circle, go round singing the three verses, and when the words "jump and spring," in the last verse, occur, the circle stops, and the joined hands are lifted up, and all the children leap out and around, on their hands and feet, (not knees,) — while the last lines are repeated twice.

In The Cuckoos, a circle is formed, or two concentric circles, and four children are put in the four corners of the room to enact cuckoos. The cuckoos sing "cuckoo," and those children in the circle answer; and when the words of the song indicate that the cuckoos should join the children, all four burst into the circle, and those who are found at their right hands become cuckoos the next time.

Almost like this last is the play of The Bees; one child being put in the corner as a drone, and at the word "*Beware*," the drone breaks into the circle.

The Wind-mill is done by dividing the children into companies of four, and letting them cross right hands and go round, and then cross left hands and go round the opposite way. By a change of the word *wind-mill* to *water-wheel*, the same music will serve for another play, in which there is a large circle formed, and then four or six spokes are made by six crossing hands in the middle, and then one or more children lengthening each spoke, and joining it to the circle, which forms the rim of the wheel. This is a more romping play than either of the foregoing, as the different velocities of those who are at the centre and circumference make it nearly impossible to have the motions correspond in time; but it is great fun, and serves for a change.

The Clappers in the Corn-mill is made by one or by two concentric circles, going round as they sing the words; and the beauty of it consists in their minding the pauses and clapping in time. Whenever there are concentric circles, as is often necessary, when there are many children, the circles should move in different directions, and all circular motions must be frequently reversed.

In The Sawyers, the children stand facing each other in couples, in a circle, and move their joined hands from shoulder to shoulder in time to the music of the first verse. In singing the second verse, they skip round with their partners.

In The Wheelbarrow, they are also arranged in couples, back to front; the front child leaning over to imitate the barrow, and stretching his hands behind him, which the child at his back takes as if to wheel. When the words are repeated the children reverse.

In The Coopers, the children, who form the barrels or hogshead, stand back to front in a circle, each taking hold of the waist of the one before him. The coopers walk round outside in time, at every third step pounding on the shoulder of the child nearest him in the barrel. When the word "around" comes, the barrel must begin to turn, and the coopers stand still, pounding on the shoulders of each child as he passes.

In The Little Master of Gymnastics, each child in turn stands in the middle of the circle, and makes any motion he chooses, which all the rest imitate.

Equal Treading is done in a circle, or in two concentric circles.

In We like to go a-roving, the children march round freely within sound of the music, singing and keeping time carefully.

In The Fishes, the children are arranged as in the pigeon-house; and at the words "swimming," "above," "below," "straight," and "bow," the fishes must make corresponding motions, while the circle that forms the pond goes round singing.

In The Pendulum, the children follow each other in a circle, moving one arm before them, like a pendulum, in time to the music, and with a strongly marked motion, while they all sing the song. When one arm is tired, the other can be used for the pendulum.

Let the children also follow one another in a circle to play THE WEATHERCOCK. Beforehand, the points of the compass should be defined in the room, and the children must point, as they sing, "North, South, East, West."

The prettiest of all the plays is THE PEASANT. All join hands and sing, going round in time with the music, when they come to the words, "Look, 'tis so — so does the peasant," they must make the corresponding motion. In the first verse, they make believe, as the children say, to hold up the apron with one hand, and throw the seed with the other. In the second verse, they kneel on one knee at the same words, and make believe hold the corn with one hand and cut with the other. In the third verse, they put the doubled fists at the left shoulder, and make the motion of thrashing. In the fourth verse, they make the motion of holding and shaking a sieve. In the fifth, they kneel on one knee and rest the head in the hand; in the sixth, they jump straight up and down, turning to each point of the compass, till the chorus, "la, la," begins, when each takes his next neighbor for a partner, and they skip round the room.

Some other plays, accompanied by musical words, can be found in the exercise books for the common schools; but there is much room for invention here, and perhaps it would be possible to put among these plays many of the national dances of the peasants of Europe.

But while the music and song will prevent disagreeable romping, care should be taken that the ease and fun of play should not be sacrificed to the music and singing. The plays must be recreation; and may often be commuted for a run in the open air, when the weather will permit.

Every day, too, it is desirable that there should be a quarter of an hour's gymnastics. Dr. Dio Lewis's free gymnastics, and his exercises with dumb-bells, rings, and wands, made small to suit infantile hands, can be alternately run through, to the sound of music. In my own Kindergarten, a graduate of Dr. Lewis's Normal School conducts these exercises; and here a considerable degree of precision can be aimed at, without danger of destroying the amusement. Children like the effect of the precision. This exercise may also occasionally be changed for a run, or for a game of bags in the open air. After some degree of skill is obtained on the dumb-bells, wands, and rings, the game of BAGS can be introduced; but at first it is alarming to little children, and it always requires so large an area, that it is best to be played in the open air.

Dancing is another exercise for the Kindergarten. In my own, I do not very rigidly give the positions and steps, but teach a simple skip forward and sideways; and then teach them ladies-chain, right and left, balancing to partners, and other simple evolutions, so that they may have cotillons and contra-dances as one form of exercise.

CHAPTER V.

BLOCKS, STICKS, AND PEAS.

FROEBEL has made a great point of block-building in his system. He invented what he has called Six Gifts, in as many different boxes. As he took infants-at-nurse into his Kindergarten, making it an object to teach mothers and nurses how to tend babies, so as to amuse them without rasping their nerves or spoiling their tempers, his First Gift was a box of six soft balls, of the primary and secondary colors; and his Second Gift a wooden ball, two cubes, and a cylinder. These gifts I shall not farther describe, as they have been published in Boston, with small manuals in each box, showing how they are to be used; and are for children in the nursery rather than in the Kindergarten.

But the other four gifts are indispensable to any Kindergarten. The Third Gift consists of eight cubes, one inch in dimension; the Fourth, of sixteen parallelopipedons two inches by one, and half an inch thick; the Fifth and Sixth, not only of such cubes and parallelopipedons, but of solid triangles, some being half the inch cube, and some a quarter of it; also cubes divided horizontally, and parallelopipedons divided lengthwise.

Froebel's plan was to have the eight cubes given to the child first; and to have him led by imitation and suggestion to make these into the forms of chairs, sofas, monuments, columns, stalls for horses, tanks, &c., &c. Also into symmetrical forms, which may be called patterns for carpets. Each box adds new material for greater varieties of form till at last quite elaborate houses can be represented, and very complicated forms of beauty. The child is to be left to his own spontaneity as much as possible, but the teacher is to suggest means of carrying out whatever plan or idea the child has. What is cultivating about the exercise is, that the child makes or receives a plan, and then executes it; has a thought, and embodies it in a form.

But something more can be done with the blocks. They can be made symbolical of the personages and objects of a story. Thus even with the eight blocks, five may be a flock of sheep, one the shepherd, one a wolf, who is seen in the distance, and who comes to steal a sheep, and one the shepherd's dog who is to defend the sheep against the wolf. When all the blocks come to be used, much more complicated dramas may be represented. The teacher should set an example, as, for instance, thus: "I am going to build a light-house, so;" (she piles up some blocks and leaves openings near the top, which she says are "the lantern part where the lights are put;" near the light-house are a number of blocks, rather confusedly laid together, of which she says,) "These are rocks, which are very dangerous for ships, but which are scarcely ever seen, because the water dashes over them, especially when there is a storm, or when the night is dark; and that is the reason the light-house is put here. Whenever sailors see a light-house, they know there is danger where it stands; and so they steer their ships away from the place. Look here! here is a ship," (and she constructs with other blocks something which she calls a ship, or schooner, or sloop, representing respectively the number of masts which characterize each kind of vessel,) "And there is a pilot standing upon it who has seen the light-house, and is turning the ship another way."

Having built her story, she will now call upon the children to build something. Some will imitate her; others will have plans of their own. As soon as one has finished, he or she must hold up a hand, and the teacher will call upon as many as there is time for, to explain their constructions. There is no better way for a teacher to learn what is in children, their variety of mental temperament and imagination, than by this playing with blocks. Some will be prosaic and merely imitative; some will show the greatest confusion, and the most fantastic operations of mind; others the most charming fancies; and others inventive genius. But there will always be improvement, by continuing the exercise; and it is a great means of development into self-subsistence and continuity of thought. In my own Kindergarten, a gifted teacher has made this block-building a means of teaching a great variety of things, and among other things, Natural History. A half an hour nearly every day is given to it. I have a table twelve feet long and four or five feet broad, and before the children come, she sets up along the length of the table, a variety of constructions, representing woods, rocks, bushes, or whatever she wants as the haunts of the animals whose habits she wishes to describe. She then invents some story, or incidents, that shall involve the facts which she means to convey. Twenty-five or thirty children can stand or kneel round the table; and when they come up, she explains what she has built, — about which they are very curious. They will listen to her for a quarter of an hour, while their eyes are filled with these blocks, which assume, to their quick imaginations, whatever form she may choose to give them, when, if she were to speak without these material things before their eyes, it would be quite impossible to command their silent attention so long. When she has done, she says, "Now you build!" and as all have boxes before them, each containing about twenty-five blocks, they immediately begin to build. What they are taught by the teacher reappears, day after day, in their constructions, mingled with circumstances of their own invention. When their stories are very fantastic, they are received by the teacher as jokes. When there is attempt to represent realities, there is opportunity for correcting erroneous impressions that have been given, and it is pretty to see how much they learn by this amusement. The teacher preserves a certain method in what she represents. She sometimes divides the table into Asia and Africa; and occasionally adds Australia, America, and Europe; and keeps her animals in their own quarter of the world. If any child has an animal in his or her story, she is asked of what country it is; and if several animals, of different countries, are in the story, a question arises of how it can be; and sometimes a menagerie is imagined to account for inconsistencies of geography. It is obvious to the slightest reflection how much can be taught in this way. But the teacher must be well posted in Natural History, and is obliged to read books of travels, &c., to get anecdotes. We have found the works of J. G. Woods, "Common Objects of the Country," "My Feathered Friends," and especially the large work he edits, called "Routledge's Illustrated Natural History," very useful.

In order to make these lessons in Natural History still more useful, we have some large cards, imported from Europe, on which birds and other animals are represented in the proportions of their size; and these are exhibited when the animals are spoken of. In order to impress the forms still more strongly, I draw the animals on paper, and let the children prick their outlines, — which forms another exercise, and is very much delighted in by the children. They thus have something to carry home which they have done themselves.

I have said that Froebel's First and Second Gifts are published in Boston. I think the other Gifts — that is the Third and Fourth, together with some of Fifth and Sixth, will presently be published in one box, with some lithographic plates of the forms they can make. For it is indispensable that every child in a Kindergarten should have a box of blocks; and the book of plates would enable them sometimes to play with the blocks when the teacher cannot be superintending them. The box and book would also be quite a resource for children at home, especially after they have learnt how to play from a good teacher. All is accomplished when the child makes a plan, embodies it, and gives an account of what he has done.

But blocks may also be used to give the elements of arithmetic and geometry, as I shall show in the proper place.

STICK-LAYING.

Barley straws can be used with much advantage to form a pleasant amusement for children. They should be cut into pieces of an inch, two inches, three inches, four inches, five inches, and six inches; and each of the children should have a hundred in a box. They can then be taught to lay them so as to make windows, doors, houses, fences, and the various rectilinear figures, regular and irregular polygons. They can make these figures with their barley-straws, and then copy them on their slates, one side of which it is a good plan to have marked with a steel point in squares of half an inch, or a third of an inch dimension; for there is nothing so hard in drawing as to make a straight line. Several of the capital letters can be made by these barley-straws, as A, E, F, H, I, K, L, M, N, T, V, W, X, Y, Z. Then these can be copied upon the slate, and the children will soon add the rest of the letters on their slates, making the curves with their pencils. Froebel used stiff wooden sticks; but I mention barley-straws, because I have found it difficult to get the straight wooden sticks.

PEA-WORK.

But hard wooden sticks, sharpened at both ends, are necessary for pea-work. The object, in this kind of work, is to make frames of houses, chairs, tables, &c., by using *peas*, first dried, and then soaked in water. The peas make points of union for the sticks. Among Froebel's gifts a box of sticks and peas is found, and it would pay any toy-dealer to get the box up in this country. The best way to prevent in children the habit of destruction, is to give them means for construction.

The first step in pea-work is, as usual, the most simple: a certain number of sticks and peas are given to the child, and the question is asked, What can you form? When the teacher has ascertained, by having heard the children's answers to her question, what is the peculiar individuality of each child, she commences with the most simple forms. She takes a stick, and places at each end a pea, and asks what is this like? The answers will be various: a candle, a pin, a pillar, the letter I, and the round of a chair. On this last hint she may proceed and form two rounds in the same way, and then set sticks in the peas at right angles, and at last unite these so as to make a square. This will become the foundation of the chair. Then four more sticks may be stuck into the same peas, vertically at right angles with the others, and these can be united by horizontal lines representing the seat of the chair. Then by means of three more sticks the outline of the back of the chair may be made. Many frames can be made on the basis of a square, among which is a barn. Again, there can be a triangle for the basis, on which can be constructed a pyramid, an obelisk, a church spire, a prism. At first a limited number of sticks can be given to each child, afterwards an unlimited number.

For this pea-work special preparation and strict order are required; the sticks must be properly pointed and graduated in length, the peas properly softened, or the child will not be benefited.

We shall append a plate to give an idea of the pea-work, and a few patterns for the weaving spoken of in the next chapter.

CHAPTER VI.

MANIPULATIONS.

Block-building, stick-laying, and pea-work follow the more violent kinds of exercise, and seem to the children only forms of playing. While the former cannot fill up more than a quarter of each hour, the latter should not do more than fill up another quarter. Some form of manipulation can take up another quarter.

First is Sewing. — On perforated board should be drawn (both sides) simple rectilinear forms, such as spades, shovels, saws, watering-pots, bee-hives, wigwams, guns, drums, barracks, the United States flag, &c., and the children will learn to use a needle and thread with great pleasure, especially if different colored threads are used. As they become more skilful, more complicated forms and cross-stitches can be taught; and by and by canvas can be substituted for the perforated board. Plain sewing can also be taught, the girls having dolls' clothes to sew, and the boys bags for their fishing-tackle, pincushions, &c.

2. Weaving. — Another quiet amusement is to weave into paper, cut for the purpose, narrow strips of card-board of different colors. Colored cards of various colors can be bought by the thousand, and cut up carefully into strips an eighth of an inch broad. Each color should be in a different compartment of the teacher's box, and the children be allowed to choose their own colors. For a time, a simple checker-work is all that can be accomplished. By and by different patterns may be proposed by the teacher for imitation by the children. It will be necessary to cut the paper into which the card-

board is to be slipped, which is a nice process, as the cuts must be very exact. Possibly it might be done by machinery. But in my own Kindergarten we have done it ourselves, doubling the paper and using the scissors, and making the cuts correspond in size with the strips of card-board. Any colored paper may be used, but I have always used white. Among Froebel's Gifts is a box of papers already cut, and strips of paper which he proposes should be slipped into thin pieces of wood and drawn through according to the pattern proposed. But we found that it was much better to have stiff slips than to have paper with the apparatus of the wooden needle.

When Kindergartens become as common as they certainly will, as soon as the method is known enough to be appreciated, prepared boxes of cut paper and slips of colored card-board will doubtless come into commerce, and boxes of perforated board, with the patterns already drawn on both sides, all ready for the needle.

3. Pricking.—Another very attractive thing is, for the teacher to draw the forms of birds and animals on paper for children to prick. They are greatly delighted to hold these pricked forms upon the window-pane, and see the lines of light which they have made, and also to see the raised work on the other side of the paper.

A teacher can easily furnish herself with a large quantity of patterns by tracing, with a fine pen, upon engineer's cambric, from "Jardine's Naturalists' Library," or, still better, from "Routledge's Illustrated Natural History," edited by Woods, the forms of beasts and birds, with more or less detail of feathers in the case of the birds. From these patterns, tracings can be made upon paper. If children are taught a good deal about the habits, &c., of birds and beasts, it will be a very good plan to choose for the pricking the forms of what has been talked about, so that they may have exact ideas of these forms; and while they are pricking, what has been taught may be brought again to their memory by the teacher. A good deal of care should be given to meet the fancies of the children, in distributing the forms to be pricked, so that the interest may be kept vivid ; and I suppose it is needless to say, that not only must they weave, prick, or sew but a quarter of an hour at a time, but they should not do all these things on the same day, or oftener than twice a week.

To make the interest of the pricking greater, I color the forms on the patterns which I make for them, according to Nature, and allow my children to have them before their eyes while they are pricking. This coloring is very simple and unshaded ; and I find that some of the children, who have paint-boxes at home, color the pricked forms, when they get home, according to their recollection of the pattern. It would be a formidable thing to undertake to superintend the coloring at the Kindergarten ; but if one had assistants enough this also could be done, at least in the case of the older ones. Newton's albumen colors, if they were a little cheaper, would serve nicely ; but, at all events, it would be a very great task for the teachers, and small children would succeed so indifferently that it is quite a question whether it would be worth while for them to attempt anything so difficult. Nothing should be undertaken, in the Kindergarten, in which there is not a fair chance of some considerable success, for it is not a good habit *to fail* in anything which is seriously attempted ; and one great reason for superintending children in what they do is, that an adult's judgment is necessary for the choice of what is attempted. The habit of success produces perseverance.

4. Paper Folding and Cutting.—This is an amusement which may lead to beautiful results. Billings, one of our most gifted artists, first developed his genius with paper and scissors. Exquisite delicacy and rich invention were displayed in his paper cuttings, even when he was but five or six years of age. Let each child be provided with a pair of scissors, and a square piece of thin paper. Also

have the same yourself, and let them imitate you, as you go through the following process :—

1. Lay the paper straight on the table. 2. Unite two opposite corners and crease the fold, which will make a triangle. 3. Hold the doubled corners in the fingers and unite the other two corners, by which a smaller triangle is produced with one side closed and the other open. 4. Turn one of the folds to the right, the other to the left, keeping the corners, where they are all united, between the forefinger and the thumb, and cut the paper at the base, so as to form an acute-angled isosceles triangle. 5. Now cut into all the creases as they are folded together, and into the edges, making little diamonds, or any kind of cuts, and gouging out small pieces. 6. Unfold, and a symmetrical pattern will be found to be cut.

These first manipulations can be easily performed by the youngest children. When done, the little figures are collected, put into an envelope, and taken home.

It can be proposed that a child should cut in paper shapes of ivy leaves, and other flowers; of birds, animals, &c. At first, models for imitation can be given; but from the first, children should be incited to invent forms. Upon a paper simply folded once, cups, vases, beautiful bowls, with two handles, can be produced; and where there is genius for producing forms of beauty, it will not fail to show itself very soon. Symmetrical forms being insured by the folding, the smallest child can accomplish something, which will please the eye and encourage to new efforts.

Paper folding can be made the means of developing geometrical power in children, as will be shown in the proper place.

5. Moulding. — This is the highest form of manipulation, and one which is very fascinating to children, who often make forms with mud and snow in their out-door play.

The material, whether clay, rice, wax, or whatever else may be employed, must be previously prepared, and always kept in a plastic state.

Clay is the least expensive material, but it must always be kept wet, and it is cold to the hands. Wax, prepared with oil, is more expensive, but far cleaner than clay; and it has the advantage of preserving the forms moulded, while the clay shrinks and cracks when it dries.

The material being prepared, each child is supplied either with a small flat board, slate, cloth, or strong paper, to cover the part of the table used; a small blunt elastic knife, and a portion of the plastic material. The child is first left to pursue the bent of its own inclinations,—generally the roller and the ball are the first objects attempted,— in their formation the child finds great delight. Irregular forms are, however, the easiest. The children are encouraged to imitate birds' nests, baskets, candlesticks, and various fruits: apples, pears, strawberries, also some vegetables, and especially flowers;— whenever it is possible let them have the natural objects before them. Afterwards models of animals are given for imitations; and they are encouraged to make parts of the human figure,— fingers, hands, ears, noses, for which they have models in each other. I have known a boy not twelve years old, who would take an engraved head, and mould one by it, in which the likeness would be remarkable;— he used wax and a pin.

To make forms from the hint of an engraving, is a little above imitation; and it is to be remembered that we do not wish the children to stop with imitations. Let them go on and invent forms, beautiful vases, pitchers, &c. When they begin to make heads and human figures, a teacher, who understands the principles of drawing, can bring to their notice the proportions of the human figure and face found in nature, which make ideal beauty. Many a heaven-destined sculptor will find himself out, in the Kindergarten.

6. Drawing and Painting.— Mr. Sheldon, in his "Elementary Instruction," has given, in detail, "Krusi's System of Inventive Drawing," which has its merits; but Miss M. A. Dwight, in the pages of "Barnard's Journal of Edu-

cation," has presented some important considerations in favor of a different method for those whose final object is Art, — and that is the object always to be aimed at.

In my own Kindergarten, I found that the lessons of Madame Rongé's Guide were so uninteresting to my children, that I abandoned that course, and got from Dr. Rimmer, the sculptor, (who has given, in his own drawing-school in Boston, a new idea of what is meant by *teaching drawing*,) some elementary sketches involving the proportions of the human figure. My assistant draws on the black-board line by line, which the children copy on their slates, very much interested, as they go on, to know what is coming.

Light-houses, cottages, barns, &c., around which are figures of men, drawn sometimes by five single, sometimes by five double lines, surmounted by a large dot for a head, and in all attitudes, particularly in attitudes of action, excite the imagination to invention, and give a freedom of hand, as well as of fancy, which, I am inclined to think, is a better beginning than geometrical lines and angles. I find that it wakes up interest in every child.

I speak, however, only of the beginnings for little children. Krusi's exercises can come by and by, and are very naturally connected with stick-laying, and make, perhaps, the only method of drawing which can be introduced into the public primary schools, where classes are so very large. Every mechanic needs such drawing lessons, as well as perspective, taught by Schmidt's practical method.

My plan is, however, more favorable to the attainment of picturesque drawing, and especially to the representation of the human figure, in which art culminates.

I have already said, that coloring cannot be easily introduced into the Kindergarten. The most advanced class, however, might connect it with the lessons on color, which are prominent in the object teaching. Paper, ruled in small squares, might be used to teach children to lay on an equal tint. First, only the smallest square should be covered, and the colors can be arranged according to the harmonies. Then four squares could be covered with one color, and so on. Ruskin's "Elements of Drawing with Colors," will furnish a teacher with good hints how to proceed. But, of course, this is not the place to give a manual of painting.

CHAPTER VII.

MORAL AND RELIGIOUS EXERCISES.

HARMONIOUS development is Froebel's idea. Hence, although the physical should never be sacrificed, and comes first into view, in the scheme of Kindergarten culture, it is not to be exclusive. Children grow in stature and physical force, all the better for having their hearts and minds opened in the beginning. It is desirable to have a child become conscious of right and wrong, in reference to eating and drinking, quite early; though temptation to excess should be removed, as a general thing, by giving them simple wholesome food. In any case where children may not go home at noon, and there is a luncheon, some simple fruit, like apples or grapes, together with milk biscuits, or plain bread and butter, make the best repast, satisfying hunger, and not stimulating the palate unduly. I am sometimes shocked at the kind of luncheon children bring to the Kindergarten, it shows such lamentable ignorance of physiological laws. The practical value of the beautiful symbol of the origin of evil, which stands as the first word of the sacred volume, is enhanced, by its having the form in which temptation first assails the child. No deeper interpretation of it is foreclosed by our presenting it at first, to children, just as it stands. The forbidden fruit is that which will hurt the child; *i. e.*, give it the disease which by and by may make death a merciful release from pains intolerable to bear. Serpents have no higher function than eating; but human beings live to know and love and do good, and so ought not to eat everything that is pleasant to the eyes, — but to stop, as Eve did not, and inquire whether it is God or the mere animal which is man's proper adviser. Our appetite is the serpent, our thought is from God. A child understands all this very early, if it is thus simply presented; and it suggests the beginning of his moral life. The lesson can soon be generalized. Whatever wrong things he is tempted to do, whatever his conscience tells him not to do, is "forbidden fruit;" his desire to do it is the serpent, and if he falls, it is the old folly of Eve, who preferred the advice of the lower being to the command of God, always given in the Conscience.

I have known a child, to whom this story was early read and interpreted, to whom it seemed to become a "guard angelic" over her life. The moral nature responded to it at once, and a suggestion that a desire was perhaps the voice of the serpent, was always quite enough to arouse the guardian angel — Conscience — to a watch and ward of the severest character. It precluded the necessity of present punishment and the fear of future retribution, (with which a child should never be terrified.)

There is such a thing as making children, I will not say too conscientious, but too conscious; and this is often done by well-meaning parents and teachers, who make them look upon themselves personally as objects of God's pleasure or displeasure. This will be avoided by using a symbol, like the story of Adam and Eve, which touches the imagination, and saves them from the reactions of personal pique. A judicious teacher, who knows how to paraphrase as she reads, and to skip what is mere prosaic statement, (and no one who cannot do this, is fit to read to children,) can make use of many other passages of the Old and New Testament, and of "Pilgrim's Progress," to give to children the whole doctrine of religious self-control, and inspire them to the highest moral issues.

Spiritual life, strictly speaking, can only be *prepared for* by the *best* education. Its characteristic and essence consists in that action of the heart and reason which does not come from human prompting. But it *can* be prepared for, by awakening in the child such an aspiration and felt necessity for virtue, as well as general idea of God, as makes prayer to the Father of Spirits spontaneous and inevitable. I am in the habit of speaking of God to children as the Giver of love and goodness, and of the power of thought and action, rather than as the Creator of the outward world, and have found that the tyrannizing unity of the soul's instinct did the rest.

I commence the exercises of the Kindergarten with the singing of a hymn, — and every other day it is the Lord's prayer, just so far transposed as to suit it to the lovely music to which it is set in this volume, and which interprets the meaning to their hearts. Now and then I ask them if "our Father's" being "in heaven" means, that He is not on earth? — and when they all say, No, (as they always do say,) I reply, "No, indeed; He is everywhere, and inside of us all, but spreads out into heaven and future time, where He is building mansions for his dear good children." As they always tell me, when I ask what *hallowed* means, that they do not know, I explain it as meaning that when we say God, we should always think and feel how dear and good He is, and speak His name with love. The *doing the will on earth as in heaven* is, as they know, acting right, and like as the angels would if they lived on earth. Conscience assures this to them, and that to do so would make the kingdom of heaven on earth. *Trespasses* I explain, showing them how, in meddling with other children's things, hurting others, or any wrong-doing, they *trespass* against God's kingdom, which is the prevalence of goodness. On being first asked what a "trespass" is, they will themselves define it very well, often by examples; and they can be led to see how wrong it is to make another do wrong, because that is "leading them into temptation." I do not let the Lord's prayer come every day, but alternate it with the song on brotherly love and other virtues. Occasionally, when there is a striking violation of the principles sung by the lips, I say to them that *doing* the right thing is the *soul's* song, which is as sweet to our heavenly Father, as the best music we can hear is to us.

All reading to children should be more or less symbolical, and calculated to elevate the imagination, whose highest use is to represent the spiritual in the forms of beauty for our moral culture. In all the child's literature, with which our book-stores are flooded, there is very little which is truly imaginative (for I draw a distinction between the fanciful and imaginative). Nothing is worthy to be called imaginative that does not involve an idea, in the strictest sense of that word. The parables of the Old and New Testaments are embodiments of ideas, and touch this master-spring of the human mind — Imagination. So is the Pilgrim's Progress; and so are many fairy tales, and many mythological stories of Greece, India, and the North. I have found an English book, called the "Heroes of Asgard," invaluable; and "The Story without an End" is a beautiful reading-book for children, in whose pages they find themselves in a maze of beautiful images and picturesque words, waking echoes that do not sleep again, but give presentiments and foretaste "of the perfect good and fair."

In my own Kindergarten, I have the advantage of a teacher who knows how to read children's characteristics of temperament and imagination unerringly, and to read to them naturally. When she reads, as she does, a quarter of an hour every day, for moral culture, she always addresses herself to the youngest of the class; and it is equally interesting to the oldest of them. If attention wanders, she calls the name of the wanderer as if she were talking, and the result is the most complete general attention. As she never goes to the reading without having previously read the lesson over to herself, the book is merely her note-book for discourse as it were. Her favorite books are fables, fairy stories, the "Heroes of Asgard," Mrs. Farrar's "Robinson Crusoe," "Sandford and Merton," "Salzmann's Elements of Morality." This exercise is very interesting to a spectator or listener. The children are drawn up close before her in a solid square, every eye seeking hers; and their spontaneous exclamations and interlocutions prove how completely she has them, heart and soul, in her keeping for the time being.

But while by this and other means, a large measure of moral and religious consciousness may be educated, we must beware of overstraining in this direction. Children who are made too conscientious become timid and morally weak, and often exhibit painful reactions. Coarse teachers often do great harm, with the best intentions, to finely strung moral organizations. Encouragement to good should altogether predominate over warning and fault-finding. It is often better, instead of blaming a child for short-coming, or even wrong-doing, to pity and sympathize, and, in a hopeful voice, speak of it as something which the child did not mean to do, or at least was sorry for as soon as done; suggesting at the same time, perhaps, how it can be avoided another time. Above all things, an invariable rule in moral education is not to throw a child upon self-defence. The movement towards defending one's self and making excuses, is worse than almost any act of overt wrong. Let the teacher always appear as the friend who is saving or helping the child out of evil, rather than as the accuser, judge, or executioner. Another principle should be, not to confound or put upon the same level the trespasses against the by-laws of the Kindergarten, made for the teacher's convenience, and those against the moral laws of the universe. The desirableness of the by-laws that we make for our convenience can be shown at times when the children are all calm, and their attention can be drawn to the subject; and if these regulations are broken, all that is necessary will be to ask if it is kind and loving to do such things? But it must never be forgotten that natural conscience always suffers when artificial duties are imposed. Hence the immoral effect of formality and superstition.

In a well-regulated Kindergarten there should be no punishments, but an understanding should be had with parents that sometimes the child is to be sent home for a day, or at least for some hours. The curtailment of the Kindergarten will generally prove an effectual restraint upon disorder, and it will not be necessary to repeat the penalty in a school year.

But I shall say no more upon moral and religious exercises, Mrs. Mann having treated this part of the subject so exhaustively. It is to be remembered, however, that she had in her school children who had strayed much farther from the kingdom of heaven than those who will generally make up the Kindergarten. But she shows the *spirit* that should pervade all that is done to children at all times.

CHAPTER VIII.

OBJECT LESSONS.

I NOW come to Object Lessons, which should begin simultaneously with all the above exercises; for mental exercises are not only compatible with physical health, but necessary to it. The brain is not to be overstrained in childhood, but it is to be used. Where it is left to itself, and remains uncultivated, it shrinks, and that is disease. A child is not able to direct its own attention; it needs the help of the adult in the unfolding of the mind, no less than in the care of its body. Lower orders of animals can educate themselves, that is, develop in themselves their one power. As the animals rise in the scale of being, they are related more or less to their progenitors and posterity, and require social aid. But the human being, whose beatitude is "the communion of the just," is so universally related, that he cannot go alone at all. He is entirely dependent at first, and never becomes independent of those around him, any further than he has been so educated and trained by his relations with them, as to rise into union with God. And this restores him again to communion with his fellow-beings, as a beneficent Power among its peers.

The new method of education gives a gradual series of exercises, continuing the method of Nature. It cultivates the senses, by giving them the work of discriminating colors, sounds, &c.; sharpens perception by leading children to describe accurately the objects immediately around them.

Objects themselves, rather than the verbal descriptions of objects, are presented to them. The only way to make words expressive and intelligible, is to associate them sensibly with the objects to which they relate. Children must be taught to translate things into words, before they can translate words into things. Words are secondary in nature; yet much teaching seems to proceed on the principle that these are primary, and so they become mere counters, and children are brought to hating study, and the discourse of teachers, instead of thirsting for them. To look at objects of nature and art, and state their colors, forms, and properties of various kinds, is no painful strain upon the mind. It is just what children spontaneously do when they are first learning to talk. It is a continuation of learning to talk. The object-teacher confines the child's attention to one thing, till all that is obvious about it is described; and then asks questions, bringing out much that children, left to themselves, would overlook, suggesting words when necessary, to enable them to give an account of what they see. It is the action of the mind upon real things, together with clothing perceptions in words, which really cultivates; while it is not the painful strain upon the brain which the study of a book is. To translate things into words, is a more agreeable and a very different process from translating words into things, and the former exercise should precede the latter. If the mind is thoroughly exercised in wording its perceptions, words will in their turn suggest the things, without painful effort, and memory have the clearness and accuracy of perception. On the other hand words will never be used without feeling and intelligence. Then, to read a book will be to know all of reality that is in it.

I am desirous to make a strong impression on this point, because, to many persons, I find object-teaching seems the opposite of teaching! They say that to play with things, does not give habits of study. They think that to commit to memory a page of description about a wild duck, for instance, is better than to have the wild duck to look at, leading the child to talk about it, describe it, and inquire into its ways and haunts! They do not see that this study of the things themselves exercises the perception, and picturesque memory, which is probably immortal, certainly perennial, while the written description only exercises the verbal memory. Verbal memory is not to be despised; but it is a consequence, and should never be the substitute for picturesque memory. It is the picturesque memory only which is creative.

There is another and profound reason why words should follow, and not precede things, in a child's memory. It will have a tendency to preclude the unconscious sophistry which takes the place of real logic in so many minds; and at all events will give the power to detect sophistry; for it necessitates the mind to demand an image, or an idea, for every word. It gives the habit of thinking things and principles, instead of thinking words merely; — of looking through rhetoric after truth and reality. There is nothing perhaps which would conduce more to sound morality and earnestness of character, in this country, than that object-teaching, as proposed in Mr. Sheldon's "ELEMENTARY INSTRUCTION," should pervade the primary schools. It would require a volume to go into object-teaching, in such detail as to serve as a manual for teachers; and happily the work of Mr. Sheldon's, just named, precludes the necessity of my doing so. It is published broadcast over our northern States; and every teacher, especially every Kindergarten teacher, should procure it, and give days and nights to the study of it, until its methods and matter are completely mastered. I have one or two exceptions to take, in respect to it myself, as will be seen in the sequel; yet I consider it not only an invaluable manual, but that it goes far to supply the place of the training school for teachers on the Pestalozzian plan, "for whose use I believe it was primarily intended."

Object-teaching should precede as well as accompany the process of learning to read. In Germany, even outside of Kindergarten, *thinking schools* have long preceded *reading schools*, and yet learning to read German, in which every sound is represented by a different letter, and every letter has one sound, cultivates the classifying powers, as learning to read English cannot. With children whose vernacular is English, it is absolutely injurious to the mind to be taught to read the first thing. I must speak of the reasons of this in another place, my purpose here being to show that object-teaching is necessary, in order to make word-teaching, whether by teacher's discourse, or by the reading of books, a means of culture at any period.

Every child should have the object to examine, and in turn each should say what is spontaneous. Out of their answers series of questions will be suggested to the teacher, who should also be prepared with her own series of questions, — questions full of answers.

The first generalization to which children should be led is into the animate and inanimate,— what lives and what exists without manifestation of life. The next generalization will be into mineral, vegetable, animal, and personal.

But you can begin with chairs, tables, paper, cloth, &c., coming as soon as possible to natural objects. Mrs. Agassiz's "First Lesson in Natural History" is an excellent hint. Sea anemones, star-fishes, clams, and oysters are easily procured. If sea anemones, taken into a bottle of salt water, clinging to stones, look like mere mosses at first, on the second day it is pretty certain, that in their desire for food they will spread themselves out, displaying their inward parts in the most beautiful manner. Every child in the class should have his turn at the object, if there are not objects enough for each, — should tell what he sees, and be helped to words to express himself. This, I must repeat, is the true way of learning the meaning of words; and leaves impressions, which no dictionary, with its periphrases and mere approximations to synonymes can give. Let a child himself hammer out some substance with a mallet, and he will never forget the meaning of malleable; and so of other words. As far as possible we should always use Saxon words, but it is the words that come from the Latin and Greek, which it is most necessary to teach the meaning of; and they should be taught by things themselves, which have them for names or qualities.

A good linguist will have an advantage here, by being able to trace the words through the original language up to nature; for every word is, in the last analysis, either a picture, whose original in nature is its definition, or a poem, which can be recognized by the general imagination. A child whose vernacular is English will easily see that a *bit* is something bitten off, and so is smaller than the mouth; but that *morsel* means a bit is not so obvious to one who does not know that *morsus*, also, is the perfect participle of the Latin verb for bite. That *acute* means *sharp* is plainer to a child who knows that *acu* is the Latin for needle.

No time is lost which is given to this definition of words by the objects of nature and art, from which, or from whose attributes, words are derived. In words are fossilized the sciences, that is, the knowledge mankind has already attained of nature; and he who understands all the words in use, would know all that is known, nay, much that has been once known and long forgotten. But the study of objects not only gives significance to words, it educates the senses, and produces the habit of original attention and investigation of nature. These do not come of themselves, as we see in the instance of country children, who are ignorant of what is around them, because left to grow up among the objects of nature, without having their attention called to things in their minutiæ, or their relations in extensu; nor led to clothe with words their perceptions, impressions, and reasonings.

Besides Mr. Sheldon's "Elementary Instruction," there is the "Child's Book of Nature," by Worthington Hooker, in three parts, which will be a great help to an object-teacher. It is published by the Harpers, and is the very best introduction of children to flowers.* Mrs. Mann's "Flower People" is also full of facts, carefully studied out. This is a charming book for children to read in, when they shall come to read. It is a great pity that the latest edition, published by Ticknor and Fields in 1862, is not illustrated by the flowers spoken of. But perhaps these may be lithographed, and published in a card-case, to accompany it. Both the science and cultivation of flowers comes very naturally into the Kindergarten.

The greatest difficulty about object-teaching is, that it requires personal training, and wide-awake attention in teachers, of a character much more thorough than they commonly have. When it shall become general, as it certainly must, it will no longer be supposed that any ordinary person who can read and write, and is obliged to do something for a living, will be thought fit to keep a school for small children! The present order of things will be reversed. Ordinary persons, with limited acquirements, will be obliged to confine themselves to older pupils, who are able to study books and only need to have some one to set their lessons and hear them recited; while persons of originality and rich culture will be reserved to discover and bring out the various genius and faculty which God has sown broadcast in the field of the race, and which now so often runs into the rank vegetation of vice, or wastes into deserts of concentrated mediocrity. Then this season of education will command the largest remuneration, as it will secure the finest powers to the work; and because such work cannot be pursued by any one person for many years, nor even for a short time without assistance, relieving from the ceaseless attention that a company of small children requires, for little children cannot be wound up to go like watches; but to keep them in order, the teacher must constantly meet their outbursting life with her own magnetic forces; while their

* Gray's *How Plants Grow*, is invaluable for a teacher.

employments must be continually interchanged, and mingled with their recreations.

Children ought to continue these Kindergarten exercises from the age of three to nine; and if faithfully taught, they could then go into what is called scholastic training, in a state of mind to receive from it the highest advantages it is capable of giving; free from the disadvantages which are now so obvious as to have raised, in our practical country, a party prejudiced against classical education altogether.

CHAPTER IX.

GEOMETRY.

REV. DR. HILL, the present President of Harvard College, in his articles in Dr. Barnard's "Journal of Education," has set forth the importance of Geometry in the earliest education, giving the Science of Form precedence to that of numbers. Of course he does not mean that logical demonstration is to form one of the exercises of little children! but that observation of differences and resemblances of shape, and the combination of forms, should be inwoven with the amusements of children. He invented a toy on the principle of the Chinese tanagram, (published by Hickling, Swan & Co., in Boston,) to further an exercise which begins in the cradle with the examination of the hands and feet.

The blocks are the first materials. Take the cube and ask how many faces it has; how many corners; and whether one face is larger than another or equal; and finally, lead the child to describe a cube as a solid figure with six equal sides, and eight corners. Then take a solid triangle from the box and draw out by questions that it has five sides and six corners, that three of its sides are equal, and two others equal; that the three larger sides are four-sided, and the two smaller sides are three-sided; and that the corners are sharper than those of a cube.

Make analogous use of all the blocks, and of the furniture of the room, of the sphere and its parts, the cylinder, &c. Do not require the definition-formulas at first, but content yourself with opening the children's eyes to the facts which the formula afterwards shall declare.

Paper-folding can be made subservient to another step, just short of abstraction.

Give each one of a class a square piece of paper, and proceed thus: What is the shape of this paper? How many sides has it? Which is the longest side? How many corners has it? Have in hand, already cut, several acute and obtuse angled triangles, and showing them, ask if the corners of the square are like these corners? If they are as sharp as some of them; or as blunt as some? Spreading out the triangle before them say, which is the sharpest corner, and which the bluntest? and let the children compare them with the corners of the square, by laying them upon the square. They will see that the square corners are neither blunt nor sharp, but as they will perhaps say, *straight.* Let them look round the room, and on the furniture and window-sashes, find these several kinds of corner. At least they can always find right angles in the furniture. Then tell them there is another word for corners, namely, *angles,* that a square corner is a *right* angle, a sharp corner a sharp angle, and a blunt corner a blunt angle.

If the teacher chooses she can go farther and tell them that *acute* is another word for sharp, and *obtuse* another word for blunt; (or these two *Latin words* may be deferred till by and by, one new word *angle* being enough to begin with.)

You can then say, "Now tell me how you describe a square, supposing somebody should ask you that did not know;" and give them more or less help to say: "A square is a figure with four equal sides and four straight corners (or right angles)." To prove to them that it is necessary to mention the right angles in describing a square, you can make a rhombus, and show them its different shape with its acute and obtuse angles. Having thus exhausted the description of a square, let every one double up his square, and so get an oblong. Ask if this is a square? What is it? How does it differ from a square? Are all four sides different from each other? Which sides are alike? How are the corners (or angles)? In what, then, is it like a square? In what does it differ? Bring out from the child at last the description of an oblong, as a four-sided figure with straight corners (or right angles), and its opposite sides equal. Contrast it with some parallelogram which is not a rectangle, and which you must have ready. Let them now fold their oblongs again, and crease the folds; then ask them to unfold and say what they have, and they will find four squares. Ask them if every square can be folded so as to make two oblongs, and then if every oblong can be so divided as to make two squares? If they say yes to this last question, give them a shorter oblong, which you must have ready, and having made them notice that it is an oblong, by asking them to tell whether its opposite sides are equal, and its angles right angles, ask them to fold it, and see if it will make two squares. They will see that it will not. Then ask them if all oblongs are of the same shape; and then if all squares are of the same shape?

The above foldings will be enough for a lesson, and if the children are small it will be enough for two lessons.

Beginning the next time, ask them what is the difference between an oblong and square? and if they have forgotten, do not tell them in words, but give them square papers and let them learn it over again as before, by their own observations. Then give them again square pieces of paper, and ask them to join the opposite corners, and crease a fold diagonally (but do not use the word diagonally). Then ask them what shape they have got? They will reply, a three-sided figure. Ask them how many corners or angles it has, and then tell them that, on account of its being three-cornered, it is called *a triangle.* Now let them compare the angles, and they will find that there is one straight corner (right angle) and two sharp corners (acute angles). Ask them if the sides are equal, and they will find that two sides are equal and the other side longer. Set up the triangle on its base, so that the equal sides may be in the attitude of the outstretched legs of a man; call their attention to this by a question, and then say, on account of this shape this triangle is called equal-legged, as well as right-angled — a right-angled equal-legged triangle. By giving them examples to compare it with, you can demonstrate to them that all right-angled triangles are not equal-legged, and all equal-legged triangles are not right-angled. Show them an equal-legged right-angled triangle, an equal-legged acute-angled triangle, and an equal-legged obtuse-angled triangle, and this discrimination will be obvious. The word *isosceles* can be introduced, if the teacher thinks best; but I keep off the Greek and Latin terms as long as possible.

Now tell the children to put together the other two corners of their triangles, laying the sharp corners on each other, and crossing the fold; unfolding their papers they will find four right-angled equal-legged triangles creased upon their square paper. Are all these of the same shape, and of the same size? Now fold the unfolded square into oblongs, and make a crease, and they will find, on unfolding again, that they have six isosceles triangles, two of them being twice as large as any one of the other four. Ask, are all these triangles of equal size? Are all of them similar in shape? leading them to discriminate the use in geometry of the words equal and similar. Can triangles be large and small without altering the shape? Then similar and equal mean differently? Are all squares similar? are all squares equal? are all triangles equal? are all triangles similar? What is the difference between a square and oblong? What is the difference between a square and a triangle? What is the difference between a square and a rhombus? What kind of corners has a rhombus? In what is a square like a rhombus? How do you describe a triangle? What is the name of the triangles you have learnt about? They will answer right-angled, equal-legged triangles. Then give them each a hexagon, and ask them what kind of corners it has? Whether any one is more blunt than another? Whether any side is greater than another? How many sides has it? And then draw out from them that a hexagon is a figure of six equal sides, with six obtuse angles, just equal to each other in their obtuseness. Having done this, direct the folding till they have divided the hexagon into six triangles, meeting at the centre. Ask them if these are right-angled triangles, and if they hesitate, give them a square to measure with. Then ask them if they are equal-legged (isosceles) triangles. They may say yes, in which case reply yes, and more than equal-legged, they are equal-*sided*. All three sides are equal, and so they have a different name, — they are called *equilateral*. Ask, what is the difference between equilateral and isosceles, if you have given them these names, and help them, if necessary, to the answer, "equilateral triangles have all the sides equal, isosceles triangles have only two sides equal." Are equilateral triangles all similar, that is, of the same shape? Are isosceles triangles all similar? and if they hesitate or say yes, show two isosceles triangles, one with the third side shorter, and one with it longer than the other two sides.

Now give to each child a square, and tell them to fold it so as to make two equal triangles; then to unfold it, and fold it into two equal oblongs. Unfold it again, and there will be seen, beside the triangles, two other figures, which are neither squares, oblongs, or triangles, but a four-sided figure of which no two sides are equal, and only two sides are parallel, with two right angles, one obtuse and one acute angle. Let all this be brought out of the children by questions. As there is no common name for this figure, name it trapezoid at once. Then let them fold the paper to make two parallelograms at right angles with the first two, and they will have two equal squares, and four equal isosceles triangles, which are equal to the two squares. Now fold the paper into two triangles, and you will have eight triangles meeting in the centre by their vertices, all of which are right-angled and equal-legged. Ask them if they are equal-sided? so as to keep them very clear of confounding the isosceles with the equilateral, but use the English terms as often as the Latin and Greek, for the vernacular keeps the mind awake, while the foreign *technical* puts it into a passiveness more or less sleepy. Then give all the children octagons, and bring out from them its description by sides and angles; and then fold it so as to make eight isosceles triangles.

Another thing that can be taught by paper-folding is to divide polygons, regular or irregular, into triangles, and thus let them learn that every polygon contains as many triangles as it has sides, less two.

Proportions can also be taught by letting them cut off triangles, similar in shape to the wholes, by creases parallel to the base. Grund's "Plane Geometry" will help a teacher to lessons on proportion, and can be almost wholly taught by this paper-folding. Also Professor Davies's "Descriptive Geometry," and Hay's "Symmetrical Drawing."

Of course it will take a teacher who is familiar with geometry to do all that may be done by this amusement, to habituate the mind to consider and compare forms, and their relations to each other. Exercises on folding circles can be added. It would take a volume to exhaust the subject. Enough has been said to give an idea to a capable teacher. Care must be taken that the consideration should be always of concrete not of abstract forms. Mr. Hill says his "First Lessons in Geometry" were the amusements of his son of five years old. Pascal and Professor Pierce found out such amusements for themselves, which had the high end of preparing them for their great attainments in logical geometry.

It must be remembered that in a Kindergarten these lessons should not be more than a quarter of an hour long, perhaps not more than ten minutes; and that the making of paper windmills and boats, fly-boxes, and other toys out of folded paper, should occasionally intervene, prompting the children to inventions of their own. Sometimes surprising applications of their geometry to these little mechanical efforts, will be made by very small people. A child of eight years of age, with whom I read over Mr. Hill's "Geometry for Beginners," for his amusement, with practical provings, in two months after invented a self-moving carriage for his sister's dolly, that would give it a ride of ten feet.

CHAPTER X.

ARITHMETIC.

NOT only a good deal of geometrical knowledge can be given to children by comparing the forms of blocks and folding paper, *before they know how to read*, but they can learn to count also. Blocks, melon-seeds, and sticks can be used. The first point is to prevent the error of their supposing that the several units of a number have different numerical names. Put down one block and say, that is one. Then take two blocks and say, there are two. Then take three and say, there are three. Tell the child to bring you two sticks; then to go and get three sticks. For a considerable time let the exercise be for a child to take out and bring to you certain numbers of blocks. You can then say 1 and 1 are 2; 1 and 1 and 1 are 3; 1 and 1 and 1 and 1 are 4; and when the number comes to be 8 or 9, you can help the child by telling him first to make the pile 2, and then to make it 3, and then to make it 4, and so on. Thus he will learn that 2 and 1 are 3, 3 and 1 are 4, &c. It will sometimes be wise to take something else than blocks to count; melon-seeds, or little sticks; and by and by they can be asked to *think* of one apple in one hand, and two apples in the other hand, and say what number of apples there would be if they were put into one pile. If there is no hurry at all, even the slowest child can be carried along in this gradual manner, without painful confusion of mind, and the life-long aversion that sometimes arises to arithmetical calculation be prevented. After children have learnt to count as far as 100, it is well to introduce multiplication, which they must see to be addition of equal numbers; and I advise that the multiplication table should be learnt perpendicularly, but without the use of figures. Thus let them say twice 1, three times 1, 4 times 1, &c.; twice 2, three times 2, 4 times 2, &c., up to 10 times 2, before it is learnt in the usual way, (twice 1, twice 2, twice 3, &c.) Let them have objects to help along at first. Thus children will learn the substance of the multiplication, addition, and subtraction tables before they learn to read. Sometimes it is necessary to postpone it, children's minds unfold so differently. We can exercise memory by repetition. But reason cannot be hurried. We should take care that the memory of results should not take the place of numerical apprehension, which is an act of reason. And written arithmetic should be postponed till the habit of mental calculation is fully formed. Warren Colburn discovered and established the method of nature in his primary book, and no variation from his principle is to be thought of. The teacher should consult Mr. Sheldon's book, which has a fine series of the earliest exercises.

Another thing that children can learn practically is the tables of measurement. Let the teacher have gill, pint, quart, and gallon measures; and let the children themselves fill up the gallon with the quart measure, the quart with the pint measure, the pint with the gill measure, till they have the table well by heart. Then let them have other vessels, of various capacity, and guess how much they will hold, and then measure and see. This is very entertaining, and educates a power. So they can have an inch measure divided into its three barleycorns; a nail divided into its inches; a quarter of a yard divided into nails; a yard divided into its feet; and learn to measure the furniture and judge of sizes. Again there can be the weights of troy weight, and of avoirdupois weight, and a pair of scales, and the children learn to weigh in their hands.

By the blocks which are divided into halves and quarters, and by these weights and measures, some idea of fractions may be given, and by means of eagles, dollars, dimes, cents, and a piece of paper representing a *mill*, the foundation of decimal numeration can be laid in the mind.

But as I have so frequently said, let the teacher beware of premature abstraction with children, and be careful, especially in geometry, of inadvertencies of expression herself. I would suggest she should always say curve and not *curved line*. A line is length in one direction; a curve always changes the direction of the instrument making it. This verbal discrimination prevents a great deal of verbiage.

CHAPTER XI.

READING.

After children's minds have been opened by object-teaching, and indeed, simultaneously with all the above-described Kindergarten employments and recreations, I begin to teach reading, which also comes legitimately within the Kindergarten culture.

But, as I have hinted before, I consider learning to read English a somewhat unfortunate process for the mind of a child. On account of the irregularity of what is called English orthoepy and orthography, the written language is a chaos — into which, when the child's mind is introduced in the usual way, all its natural attempts at classification are baffled. The late Horace Mann, in a lecture on the alphabet, has with great humor and perspicacity shown this; and he recommended that children should be taught to read by *words* purely. But when some years afterwards his attention was drawn to the phonic method, he accepted it fully; and wrote for Mrs. Mann the preface to her Philadelphia edition of the Primer of Reading and Drawing. This was not until after it had been tested in his own family and some others, where I had introduced the phonic method.

On the details of my method I must enlarge all the more, because I find myself differing in some respects from Mr. Sheldon's plan, which loses a large part of the advantages of the phonic method by not having one definite sound for each letter. As I have taught on my plan successfully for fifteen years, I am prepared to defend it at all points, from the ground of a various experience. But I can adduce also the highest philologic authority for my mode of sounding the alphabet,* as well as an argument of common sense from the nature of the case.

The primal cause of the chaotic condition of English orthography, is the fact that the Roman alphabet, which was a perfect phonography of the old Latin language, lacked characters for four English vowels and four English consonants. The Latin monks had not the wit to invent new characters for these additional sounds; but undertook to use the Roman letters for them also. Hence for the vowel heard in the words irk, err, work, and urge, they used indifferently all four characters; for truly one would do as well as another. But if they had put a dot into the middle of the o, and added it to the alphabet, it would have been better than either. Also, if for the vowel sound of pun, they had put a dot under the u; and for the vowel sound of man, they had put a dot under the a; and for the vowel sound of not, a dot under the o; they would have had four more letters in their alphabet, which would have completed the phonography of the English vowels. Similar dots under d t s c would have made a phonography of consonants, and avoided the awkward combinations of sh, ch, and the ambiguity of th, which now stands for the differing initials of *then* and *thin*.

But as they did not do this, a certain divorce took place between the ideas of the sounds and the letters; and hence the long uncertainty of the English orthography, and the stereotyped absurdities which now mark it.

It is so nearly impossible to remedy a difficulty which has passed into print so largely, that we have to accept the evil, and remedy as best we may the disadvantage it is to young minds to have all this confusion presented to them on the threshold of their literary education.†

* See the *North American Review* of January and April — articles *Kraitsir's Significance of the Alphabet*, from the pen of an eminent philologist; also Kraitsir's *Nature of Language and Language of Nature*, published in 1851, by George P. Putnam in New York.

† The only possible advantage the present spelling has, is the help it

It was suggested to me by Dr. Kraitsir, that I should take a volume of any book, and count the times that each of the vowels, and c and g, were sounded as the Romans sounded them, and how many times they were sounded otherwise, and thus see whether it was true, as he said, that these Roman sounds were the most frequent, even in the English language. I did so on a few pages of Sir Walter Scott's novels, and found that the letter i sounded as in *ink* 240 times, to one that it sounded as in *bind;* and though the proportion was not quite so great with any other vowel, yet there was a large majority for the Roman sound, in each instance, as well as for the hard sounds of c and g. Indeed I found g was hard, even before e and i, in the case of every Saxon word; and that all the soft gs, which are not many, were derived from the Norman-French.

I then set myself to find what words in English were written entirely with the Roman-sounding letters; and, to my surprise, found a large number, — enough to fill a primary spelling-book; — while most of the syllables of the rest of the words in the language yielded on analysis the same sounds. It immediately occurred to me to begin to teach children to read by these words, whose analysis would always yield them the Roman sounds, and reserve, till afterwards, the words which are exceptions, leaving the anomalies to be learnt by rote.

I tried my first experiment on a child a little more than four years old, by printing on a black-board certain words, letter by letter, until he had learned the whole alphabet, both to know each character at sight, and to print it on the black-board, and it was a signal success.

For the convenience of those who do not know the old Roman pronunciation of Latin, for which our alphabet is a perfect phonography, I will give the sounds of the letters here.

gives to Etymologists, but it also often confuses them. A perfect alphabet, that is, an alphabet with eight more characters than the Roman, would have been the right thing to have had in the right place and time.

In the case of the vowels (*voice letters*),

i	is pronounced	ĭh	as in ink,	(not eye.)
e	"	ĕh	as in ell,	(not as in be.)
a	"	ăh	as in arm,	(not as in may.)
o	"	oh	as in old,	
u	"	ŭh	as in ruin,	(not as in unit.)

in the case of the consonants, giving the power of the letter by making them finals, and obscuring the e as much as possible for the lip letters, ĕb, ĕf, ĕp, ĕv, while the semi-vowels m, n, l, r, require not even the obscure ĕ to their being sounded perfectly, shutting the lips and sounding m, opening them and shutting the palate to sound n, holding the tongue still to sound l, shaking it to sound r, (ĕl, ĕm, ĕn, ĕr;) the tooth letters ĕd, ĕt, ĕss, ĕzz — and the throat letters ĕc, ĕk, eq,* eg, and a breathing from the throat for h. Often children will come to the Kindergarten knowing the letters, in which case it is best to begin with the letters according to the organs, as is suggested in my first chapter, and when they give the old names — you can say, "No, I do not want that name but the sound."

The whole alphabet in order will then be ăh, ĕb, ĕc, ĕd, ĕh, ĕf, ĕg, h (breathed), ĭh, ĕj, ĕk, ĕl, ĕm, ĕn, ŏh, ĕp, ĕq, ĕr, ĕss, ĕt, ŭh (oo) ĕv, w (breathed) ĕx, y, just like ĭh, and not called wye, ĕz. Also the sign & for the word *and.*

In the first chapter of this book, I have detailed one method of beginning with a class, — that of giving the sounds of the letters first, classed according to the organs.

But my common way is to begin with whole words, which are more sure to interest a child. A limited number of

* k, q, and y were not Roman letters but Greek ones, k being introduced into the Latin originally as an abbreviation of ca and q as an abbreviation of cu. J and x were introduced into our alphabet by the first printers, but we have appropriated j to a new sound, not in the Latin language; and we have two sounds for x, (as printed Latin has), one being gs and the other cs. The Latins at first wrote lex legs, and vox vocs, as we see by the variations of these nouns for case.

words arranged in sentences, teaches them to know and write the whole alphabet. For the convenience of teachers who may not have either my "First Nursery Reading-Book," or Mrs. Mann's "Primer of Reading and Drawing" on hand, I will give here some sentences that contain the whole alphabet, which the teacher can teach by printing them on the black-board, and letting the children imitate them with pencil on the slate, or chalk on the black-board.

O puss, puss, pussy; O kitty, kitty, kitty; Kitty sings miu, miu; pussy sings mieaou; pussy is old, pussy is cold; put pussy into mamma's basket; mamma is singing to papa; papa is kissing mamma; pussy, go to kitty, go, go, go; kitty is in mamma's basket; go into mamma's garden, and pick roses, anemones, tulips, and pinks; mamma's velvet dress fits well; bells ring and cars go; cars go very quickly; hens sit; hens eggs; eggs in lark's nest; eggs in linnet's nest; larks sing tralala, tralala; fill mamma's basket full of roses, anemones, pinks, tulips, crocuses; Lizzy is dizzy, very dizzy; Helen is rosy red; Alexis sent his mamma a jar full of jelly; Barbara kisses Cora; Dora is spinning yarn; Flora is spinning yarn; Gilbert sent Henry a jar of guava jelly; Isabella is kissing Julia; Karlito sent a linnet's egg to Lilian; Margaret picks roses; Nina picks tulips in Olivia's garden; Penelope plants pinks in Ellen's garden; Rosalind sings to Quasi-modo; Susan puts eggs into mamma's basket; Tina brings roses to Vivian; Willy brings crocuses to mamma.

The above sentences, written over and over again, will teach all the letters; others must be added, but after certain letters are learnt, it is useful, and a pleasant variety, for the children to write columns of words, with only one letter differing; thus, old, cold, fold, gold, hold, sold, told, wold; ell, bell, dell, fell, hell, quell, sell, tell, well; art, cart, dart, hart, mart, part, tart, start; in, binn, din, fin, jin, kin, pin, sin, tin, win, &c., &c.

My "First Nursery Reading-Book" is entirely made up of such columns, after half a dozen pages of words in sentences;

and long before the children have written it half through, they can pronounce the words on first sight, though many of them are five and six syllables long.

And here I must foreclose some criticisms which have been made on this book.

First, — that the sentences are not interesting or important. That is of no moment. Children are interested in separate words ; especially if they are to write them as well as read them. I have never seen children tired of the words, and of making them.

Some persons have disputed the pronunciation of some of the words. There are, perhaps, half a dozen inadvertencies in the book which can be corrected in a second edition.

I indicate no difference between the s when it is sounded sharp, and when soft like z. But I think this will never lead to any practical error; because the language is vernacular, and the child has a teacher.

I affirm that the article *a* is sounded ah in the *spoken* language, for it is not accented. Also that in such words as deject, reject, &c., the two e's sound alike, like most unaccented e's in the language.

For a time, there is no need for the children to have a book at all. Let them have a lesson fifteen minutes long in which they write the words after the dictation of the teacher.

Let the written words remain on the black-board, and after some other employments have intervened, let them read the words off the black-board.

When they have mastered all the letters, it is a good plan to give them the book, and let them find the words. Showing them a line, ask them to look along and find a certain word.

They will be pleased to find that they can read in a book, and will like to copy on their slates the columns of words, which may be made another exercise of a quarter of an hour. In my Kindergarten, they write the words, after the teacher, on their black-boards ; and afterwards write out of the printed books upon the slate. I have hitherto had more time, in proportion, given to the reading than my own judgment quite approves; because parents are so urgent, and measure their children's progress so exclusively by their power of reading; and, if they do not learn a great deal faster than children usually learn to read, distrust the system, and interfere.

Even if this method did prove longer than other methods of learning to read, I should wish to pursue it, because to find that the same letter always represents the same sound, cultivates the mind's power of classification, and gives it confidence in its own little reasoning. But I have found that it is a shorter, not a longer, process. I have known a child of three years old, who was found to know how to read, when there was no thought of teaching him, but his brother of five years old had been taught to read upon the black-board in his presence. A child of seven years old learnt to read and write print beautifully, in three months, in lessons of ten minutes, given only when she asked for them. And in those cases there was not the additional advantage of a class. Several children in my own Kindergarten, in my first season, when I never gave half an hour in the day to reading, not only mastered my first Nursery Reading-Book, but got upon the anomalous words, and learnt to read so far, that the second season they could read fluently. If as much time was given, in the Kindergarten, to mere reading, as is given in the public schools, they would, doubtless, have learnt in three months, but I would not give the time; for I believe it is so much better for the whole nature, *i. e.*, all the powers of sense and apprehension, to be cultivated by examining objects.

I have also another difficulty to contend with. Children are taught their letters at home, and the parents interfere to help, and really hinder by bringing in the old sounds of the letters and the anomalous words, before I am ready for them. There is no objection to the children's having the

First Nursery-Book at home to use and copy on their slates, provided those at home will confine themselves to pronouncing the words to them instead of attempting to spell them.

The question, however, comes at last, But how are they to attain the rest of the language? Before I had any experience, I myself thought this was to be a great difficulty. In the first instance, after I had brought my little pupil to the point that he could print correctly any word that I pronounced to him, and could read at sight any of my selected words, I gave him a piece of poetry to read, beginning —

"Sleep, baby, sleep."

He read it *slay-ape bahby, slay-ape.*

I said, "No, that first word is *sleep.*" He was surprised, and wondered why it was written so.

I said, "Perhaps they used to say *slayape*, but they say *sleep* now; and in books there are a good many such words. Now I will rub out sl (I pronounced this combination with one impulse of the voice) and put a *w*, and say, now, what is that?" "O, That is *weep.*" Now I rubbed out the *w*, and put *d.* He immediately said, "That is deep." I said, "Now you write sleep, and under it put weep, deep, peep, keep, steep, sweep, creep." He did so, at once, and then he took great pleasure in getting a paper and lead-pencil, and writing the whole column, which, of course, he never forgot. I proceeded in the same manner, till he had not only written all the song, but all the analogues of each word, — and it was wonderful how soon he could read. The scientific habit of mind which was attained by classing the words as he learned them, has shown itself throughout his education. He never learned a so-called spelling-lesson, but he scarcely ever wrote a word wrongly spelled; and it has been a uniform observation that children taught on this method always write without errors. Each variation from the standard so strongly fixed in their minds makes a great impression; and to write the words in groups, makes these anomalies remembered in groups.

In my own Kindergarten, I give to my class "Mother Goose's Melodies." They know many of them by heart; but I make them sit in class, and each, in turn, read one word, in order to teach them to keep the place, and when they finish a verse, I ask them to find some word, and often make it the nucleus of a group of words of the same kind, to be written upon the black-board and slates as above. But I think it is a good plan, before giving a book, to call their attention to the initial sounds of *thin, then, shin, chin,* and ask them what letter stands for these. Of course they will say they do not know. Then you can say "There is none; for the people who made these letters did not have these sounds in their language; and so, when they came to write English, they put a *t* and *h* together to stand for one sound; and *c* and *h* for another; and *s* and *h* for another."

Lists of words should then be dictated and written: such as thin, think, thing, thrift, thrill, thick, bath, lath, doth, sloth, quoth, pith, smith, fifth, filth, width, depth, tenth, truth, thresh, threshold, methodist, synthetic, pathetic, cathartic, then, them, with, this, hither, thither, nether, tether, hitherto, farthing, withhold, brethren, char, chart, charm, chaff, chant, larch, march, parch, starch, chest, chess, chin, chick, chill, chit, chink, chintz, rich, chirrup, inch, pinch, clinch, flinch, winch, finch, filch, milch, clinch, trench, bench, wrench, quench, shin, ship, sharp, shark, shed, shell, shelf, shaft, shorn, shred, shrift, shrimp, shrill, flesh, mesh, fresh, dish, fish, wish, harsh, marsh, sheriff, shiver, relish, cherish, perish, freshet, finish, prudish, bluish, garnish, tarnish, varnish, blemish, refresh. Attention can then be called to the words beginning with *wh,* which are pronounced (as they were *written* in Saxon) by uttering the *h* before the *w;* as when, whet, whelk, whelp, whelm, wherry, whiz, whig, whip, whiff, whist, whisk, whirl, which, whimper, pronounced hwen, hwet, &c.

I suppose I need not say that the consideration of one of the extra consonants will be enough for one lesson.

The next step is to learn the diphthongs, that is, the proper — which I consider the only — diphthongs. Make the children pronounce oi, and see that two sounds are slid together; and then let them write on their slates, in different columns, boil, coil, foil, soil, toil, moil, spoil, coin, join, groin, point, joint, joist, hoist, foist, moist, cloister, surloin, exploit, void, &c.; also boy, coy, joy, toy, cloy, loyal, royal, envoy, enjoy, &c.

Then let them pronounce the diphthong *ou*, and write in one column the words out, our, thou, loud, proud, cloud, noun, bound, found, hound, mound, pound, round, sound, wound, bout, clout, flout, lout, gout, pout, rout, sprout, spout, shout, snout, stout, mouth, south, couch, crouch, slouch, pouch, vouch, roundabout, bounty, county, amount, abound, scoundrel, discount, expound, about, &c.; and in another, how, cow, bow, mow, now, vow, owl, scowl, brow, prow, howl, gown, brown, crown, drown, cowl, fowl, crowd, clown, frown, vowel, towel, trowel, prowess. Call attention to the proper diphthong, which we write with what we call i long, (but it is no sound of ĭh at all,) and which the Romans wrote as a diphthong with two letters, ae and ai, pronouncing it as we do the i in ire. Then let them write in columns bind, find, grind, hind, blind, kind, mind, rind, wind, violet, dialect, inquiry, horizon, &c.

This same diphthong is also written with the Greek y, — in my, thy, cry, try, fry, wry, fly, ply, asylum, dynasty, petrify, signify, vilify, vivify, simplify, rectify, edify, notify, &c.

Call attention lastly, to the diphthong yu, written first with the letter u simply, as in unit, humid, fuel, cubic, stupid, putrid, mutual, funeral, singular, bitumen, acumen, nutriment; and secondly with ew, as few, chew, pew, new, mew, mewl, eschew, sinew; thirdly with iew, as view; fourthly with eu, as in eulogy, European, &c.; sometimes with eau, as in beauty and its compounds.

There is no propriety in calling *au* a diphthong, as it is one sound, and not two sounds. It is one of the extra vowels of the English language, written when short with o (though it is no sound of o proper) a, aw, and oa.

And now we come to the consideration of the extra vowels, beginning with this sound heard short in *not*, and long in the name of a carpenter's tool, awl.

Explain that there is no character for this vowel in the Roman alphabet, because the sound was not in the Latin language, and then proceed to show how it is written in various ways: first with an o, as in bob, cob, fob, gob, job, mob, nob, rob, sob, cock, dock, hock, lock, clock, flock, mock, pock, frock, rock, crock, shock, sock, cod, hod, nod, pod, odd, shod, rod, sod, trod, doff, off, of, (pronounced ov,) cog, dog, fog, hog, jog, log, nog, doll, loll, poll, on, don, ton, pond, fond, blond, won, fop, drop, crop, lop, mop, pop, sop, top, chop, shop, stop, swop, prop, ox, box, fox, pox, moth, loth, froth, broth, lot, cot, dot, got, hot, jot, not, pot, rot, sot, tot, wot, grot, clot, shot, spot, boss, cross, dross, floss, loss, moss, toss, gloss, cost, frost, lost, tost, bond, fond, pond, pomp, romp. Then show that it is written sometimes with an a, as in all, fall, call, hall, gall, tall, wall, small, stall, ball, thrall, squall, squash, squad, squat, quart, war, dwarf, scald, bald, salt, halt, swab, ward, sward, warn, warp, warm, wand, want, was, wast, wash, swan, watch, swamp, waltz, wasp; sometimes with *au*, as in daub, fraud, gaudy, fault, vault, paunch, craunch, laurel, haul, caul, maul, augury, autumnal; and sometimes with *aw*, as in caw, daw, draw, haw, hawk, jaw, law, maw, paw, claw, straw, raw, thaw, squaw, saw, flaw, awl, shawl, bawl, brawn, drawn, awning, tawny, awkward, tawdry, sawyer, mawkish, lawful; also with oa in broad.

Another extra vowel, heard in the word man, is written, in default of a character for it, with a, as in cab, dab, gab, jab, nab, hack, back, jack, lack, pack, rack, crack, clack, black, bad, gad, glad, had, lad, mad, pad, sad, shad, bag, cag, fag, gag, hag, lag, nag, rag, crag, shag, sag, tag, wag, mall, shall, am, dam, flam, ham, sham, jam, an, ban, can, fan, clan, man, pan, ran, band, hand, land, stand, strand, grand, brand, cap, flap, gap, chap, lap, clap, map, nap, pap, sap, tap, at, bat, cat, fat, gat, hat, that, mat, pat, rat, brat, sat, spat, sprat, tat, vat. This same vowel is heard in the word plaid.

A third extra vowel is heard in *pun*, and written generally with an u; as cub, dub, hub, nub, rub, scrub, drub, tub, buck, duck, luck, cluck, muck, pluck, suck, stuck, truck, tuck, chuck, bud, cud, dud, mud, suds, stud, scud, buff, cuff, luff, bluff, muff, puff, stuff, ruff, scuff, bug, dug, drug, hug, jug, lug, slug, shrug, mug, snug, tug, cull, dull, gull, hull, mull, null, scull, gum, hum, drum, glum, plum, mum, rum, sum, bun, dun, gun, pun, run, sun, tun, stun, shun, up, cup, sup, bump, crump, dumps, gump, hump, jump, lump, mumps, pump, rump, us, buss, fuss, muss, rush, crush, gush, hush, mush, tush, bust, dust, gust, just, lust, must, rust, crust, but, cut, gut, hut, jut, nut, rut, tut, bunk, funk, sunk, drunk, trunk, hunt, put, blunt, grunt, brunt, lunch, bunch, hunch, munch, punch, bulk, sulk, skulk, gulp, pulp, gulf, tuft, bung, hung, lung, clung, rung, stung, swung, strung, musk, rusk, dusk, tusk, busk, mulct, buskin, musket, runlet, bucket, public. This same sound is written with o in mother, brother, some, come, &c., and ou in touch, and in rough, tough, enough, in which *gh* sounds like ff.

The fourth extra vowel in English having no character for it is written, first, with i, as irk, shirk, dirk, kirk, mirk, quirk, bird, gird, whirl, quirl, girl, firm, first, chirp, shirt, sir, fir, stir, flirt, spirt, squirt, squirm, girdle, &c. Secondly, with e, as in err, her, herd, term, fern, pert, wert, overt, clerk, sperm, stern, insert, vermin, perhaps, perplex, persist, expert, divert, superb, sterling, verdict, pervert, ferment, fervent, servant, perfect, serpent, partner, sever, several, inter, internal, fraternal, paternal, maternal, external, infernal, interdict, intermix, infer; and generally the final er, as silver, toper, &c. Thirdly, this vowel is written with o, as in work, worm, word, worst, world, worth; and the final or, as in arbor, ardor, vigor, &c. Fourthly, with an *u*, as in urn, burn, turn, churn, spurn, cur, fur, blur, bur, purr, spur, curb, suburb, surd, curd, surf, scurf, turf, turk, lurk, curl, furl, hurl, hurdle; and the finals ur, or, and ture, as arbor, honor, perjure, injure, &c.

Another anomaly of English orthography is the silent e, at the end of so many words; as doe, foe, hoe, roe, toe, cue, clue, blue, glue, flue, give, live, lucre, axle, noble, ogle, reptile, fertile, sterile, sextile, flexible, futile, missile, famine, jasmine, destine, pristine, frigate, senate, reptile, legate, pensive, missive, active, captive, festive, motive, sportive, illusive, defective, objective, elective, invective, perspective, defensive, expensive, preventive, retentive, progressive, vindictive, restrictive, instinctive, descriptive, explosive, corrosive, delusive, exclusive, inclusive, preclusive, intensive, palliative, narrative, relative, privative, lucrative, intuitive, infinitive, explicative, figurative, imitative, indicative, superlative, diminutive, retrospective, barnacle, spectacle, miracle, pinnacle, article, particle, ventricle, edible, credible, flexible, audible, enoble, ignoble, sensible, senile, juvenile, feminine, eglantine, multiple, dissemble, assemble, quadrille, clandestine, intestine, determine, illumine, calibre, ferule, marble, pebble, treble, tremble, nibble, quibble, scribble, nimble, meddle, peddle, kindle, spindle, fiddle, riddle, griddle, quiddle, middle, twinkle, gargle, single, mingle, sparkle, speckle, sickle, tickle, trickle, dimple, simple, pimple, ripple, triple, pickle, grizzle, little, brittle, spittle, whittle, nettle, settle, kettle, startle, tinkle, sprinkle, valise, marine, ravine, machine, Alexandrine, creditable, and other words having the final syllable *ble.*

This silent e final is found also in words which have the diphthong i; as bide, glide, hide, chide, ride, side, slide, tide, wide, bride, fife, life, wife, rife, strife, bribe, jibe, dike, like, bile, file, mile, pile, tile, vile, wile, smile, while, style, dime, time, mime, chime, rime, prime, crime, dine, fine, thine, line, nine, mine, pine, spine, shine, wine, swine, twine, vine, kine, chine, pipe, wipe, ripe, gripe, snipe, tripe, stripe, type, vie, dire, fire, hire, mire, shire, sire, tire, lyre, wire, spire, squire, tribe, scribe, bribe, jibe, bite, kite, mite, smite, kite, write, white, trite, wise, lithe, blithe, writhe, strive, thrive, drive, wive, alive, size, prize, agonize, paralyze, sympathize, symbolize, &c.

E may also be considered silent, it is so obscure, in many words ending in el and en; as harden, bidden, golden, garden, sicken, quicken, thicken, stricken, broken, spoken, token, swollen, stolen, open, kitten, mitten, smitten, bitten, given, molten, driven, woven, frozen, mizzen, dizzen, tinsel, morsel, swivel, drivel, novel, model, level, bevel, eleven, seven, &c.

U and e are both silent in the words rogue, brogue, fugue, eclogue, prologue, apologue, epilogue, intrigue, fatigue, synagogue, demagogue, pedagogue, decalogue, catalogue, mystagogue, picturesque, burlesque, grotesque, pique, casique.

U is silent in guess, guest, guard, gaunt, flaunt, taunt, daunt, avaunt, launch, staunch, laundry, laundress, liquor, piquet, coquette, paroquet, exchequer, palanquin, guarantee, gauntlet, saunter, guilt, guitar, built, build, biscuit, four, pour, court, gourd, mould, bourn, soul, moult, shoulder, poultry, coulter; and w final, when preceded by vowels, ex-except when ow stands for ou diphthong, is silent.

I is silent in fruit, suit, recruit, bruise, cruise, heifer, surfeit, forfeit, counterfeit, Madeira, and y in they, prey, whey, obey, heyday, convey, survey, purvey.

W is silent in bow, low, mow, row, sow, tow, slow, blow, glow, flow, snow, row, crow, grow, throw, bowl, own, blown, flown, grown, sown, mown, growth, owner, toward, below, lower, owner, disown, arrow, barrow, farrow, harrow, marrow, fallow, gallows, hallow, shallow, sallow, tallow, bellow, fellow, yellow, shadow, burrow, furrow, billow, pillow, willow, widow, minnow, winnow, follow, hollow, morrow, sorrow.

A is silent in boat, coat, goat, doat, moat, groat, bloat, throat, loath, oath, boast, coast, roast, coax, hoax, oak, soak, cloak, coach, poach, roach, broach, goad, load, coal, foal, goal, shoal, oaf, loaf, foam, loam, roam, loan, moan, groan, soap, oar, boar, soar, board, hoard, hoarse, hoary, cocoa, gloaming, encroach, reproach, approach.

The silent consonants are k before n — (doubtless pronounced in Saxon times,) in knit, knee, knell, kneel, knave, knife, knack, know, knead, knives, knock, knuckle.

Also, g before n, as gnat, gnaw, gnarl, gnome, gnash, reign, deign, sign, consign, assign, design, condign, benign, impugn, oppugn, arraign, campaign.

Also, g before m, as phlegm, paradigm, &c.

Also, ch in schism and drachm.

Also, l before m, k, v, f, and d — as in alms, balm, calm, qualm, calf, half, talk, balk, stalk, chalk, walk, folks, salve, halves, calves, could, would, should, almond, salmon.

Also, p before s, and sh, as in pshaw, pseudo, psalm, psalter.

Also, b before t, as debt, doubt, subtle, indebted, undoubted, &c.

And b after m is silent, as lamb, jamb, climb, tomb, womb, numb, thumb, crumb, dumb, plumb, comb, hecatomb, catacomb, currycomb, coxcomb, succumb.

Also, n after m, as column, solemn, autumn, condemn, hymn, &c.

And d before t in stadtholder.

K is often unnecessarily used after c, and t before ch.

T after s is silent in listen, glisten, hasten, chasten, christen, fasten, moisten, thistle, whistle, bristle, castle, nestle, pestle, gristle, jostle, justle, hustle, bustle, rustle, epistle, apostle, mistletoe, forecastle.

C after s is silent in scion, scent, scythe, muscle, sceptre, science, sciatica, sciolism, scissure, scission, scissors, scenery, transcend, descend, descent, viscid, crescent, proboscis, fascinate, viscera, ascetic, excrescence, corpuscle, acquiesce, coalesce, rescission, abscission, putrescence, ascendency, susceptible, irascible, viscidity, eviscerate, lascivious, resuscitate, scimitar, scintillate, phosphoresce, deliquesce, effloresce, effervesce, transcendent, condescend, condescension, convalescence, concupiscence, reminiscence, acquiescent, iridescent, arborescent, susceptibility, scenography, sciography.

The initial h is often silènt, as in hour, herbage, huge, honest, honor, humor; also, after r, rhomboid, rheum, rhyme, myrrh, ghost, aghast, catarrh, rhubarb, catarrhal, rheumatic, dishabille, rhapsody, posthumous, hemorrhage, &c.

W is silent before r in wry, write, writhe, wrath, wreath, wreathe, wrong, wretch, wright, wrist, wriggle, wrinkle; and before h in who, whose, whom, whoop, whole.

What is especially puzzling about the English orthography, is the unnecessary use of the same letter for different sounds. Thus s does not always sound s — but sometimes sounds like z. (If all the sounds z were written z, it would make our language look as full of z's as the Polish.)

After all the sonorous labials, gutturals, and dentals, we cannot help sounding z — as cabs, hods, rags, etc.; also, before m, as heroism, paroxysm, somnambulism, materialism, &c.; in monosyllables ending with a single s, as is, was, as, has, his, hers, ours, theirs; also, in daisy, reside, desire, noisy, bosom, visage, closet, resign, music, prison, reason, pansy, tansy, disown, preside, pleasant, peasant, prosaic, present, presence, Tuesday, measles, cosmos, pleasure, measure, treasure, leisure, disclosure, enclosure, composure, kerseymere, resolute, devisor, revisal, reprisal, basilisk, deposit, courtesan, raspberry, residue, venison, disaster, division, plausible, feasible, basilicon, presbytery, resolute, deposit, president, visionary, perquisite, exquisite, composite, resentment, carousal, espousal, disposal.

Instead of c or k we have in many words ch — as Christ, chasm, chyle, conch, chrome, ache, scheme, school, chaos, epoch, chorus, chronic, echo, anchor, tetrarch, trochee, archives, scholar, schooner, monarch, hierarch, chronicle, chrysalis, technical, mechanic, patriarch, pentateuch, bacchanal, saccharine, chamomile, eucharist, character, archetype, orchestra, catechize, catechism, alchemy, chemistry, schedule, paschal, chaldee, stomach, lilach, sumach, chimera, heptarchy, lachrymal.

All the above words are from the Greek, and so are those

in which f is written with ph, as sylph, lymph, sphere, sphinx, graphic, phalanx, phantom, orphan, dolphin, camphor, pamphlet, sulphur, zephyr, hyphen, trophy, philter, phaeton, spheroid, alphabet, emphasis, prophesy, prophecy, caliphate, sophistry, &c.

The sound of s is substituted for the Latin guttural (hard c) in acid, placid, facile, tacit, process, precinct, docile, recipe, illicit, cinder, fleecy, census, pencil, precept, accede, recede, concede, cite, pacify, lacerate, macerate, taciturn, oscillate, precede, implicit, explicit, decimal, precipice, specify, specimen, abbacy, imbecile, indocile, solicit, felicity, atrocity, ferocity, rapacity, tenacity, veracity, vivacity, voracity, audacity, precocity, simplicity, lubricity, rusticity, municipal, medicinal, rhinoceros, publicity, diocesan, mendacity, mendicity, duplicity, elasticity, pertinacity, incapacity, electricity, multiplicity, authenticity, duodecimo, anticipates, necessary, countenance, abstinence, and all other words which end in ce.*

The sound of j is substituted for that of g (the sonorous guttural) in germ, genus, genius, angel, gentile, pigeon, dungeon, surgeon, sturgeon, bludgeon, curmudgeon, sergeant, pageant, vengeance, stingy, dingy, &c., manger, danger, stranger, religion, badger, budget, gibbet, giblets, allegiance, plagiarism, gibe, (sometimes and better jibe;) all words ending in ge, as bilge, huge, barge, large, and all ending in dge, as wedge, ledge, pledge, hedge, sledge, fledge, ridge, bridge, midge, drudge, judge, lodge; all words ending gious, as prodigious, egregious, sacrilegious, &c.; or in geous, as courageous, &c.; or in age, as cottage, plumage, foliage, &c.

The extra consonant which we sometimes write sh, is written variously; 1st, simply with s, as in sugar, sensual, and sure, and its compounds; 2dly, with ss, in cassia; 3dly,

* Nearly every one of these words are derived from the Latin, but they come into the English language from the Norman-French in which they were already corrupted. All nouns in ce are from Latin nouns in tia, and ought to have been written with se instead of ce, except peace and voice, which come from the Latin pace and voce.

with ci, in magician, logician, patrician, optician, musician, academician, geometrician, mathematician; and in a multitude of words ending in ious, as specious, gracious, spacious, avaricious, auspicious, pertinacious, judicious, suspicious, loquacious, audacious, sagacious, fallacious, capacious, rapacious, tenacious, delicious, malicious, pertinacious, officious, capricious, ferocious, atrocious, precocious, voracious, veracious, and perhaps some others; also, in words ending with al, as official, judicial, provincial, commercial, artificial, beneficial; and in sociable, associate, appreciable and appreciate, enunciate, dissociate, excruciate, depreciate, emaciate, denunciate, renunciate, prescient, omniscient; 4thly, with ce, in cetaceous, filaceous, herbaceous, caduceous, cretaceous, testaceous, crustaceous, argillaceous, gallinaceous; 5thly, with ti, in factious, fractious, captious, vexatious, facetious, licentious, factitious, propitious, flagitious, nutritious, expeditious, superstitious, adventitious; vitiate, expatiate, ingratiate, insatiate, initiate; partial, martial, nuptial, initial, essential, substantial, credential, potential, prudential, solstitial, impartial, penitential, equinoctial, influential, reverential, pestilential, providential, circumstantial, ratio, and all words ending in tion, as ration, nation, station, notion, diction, fiction, friction, fraction, potion, action, junction, suction, section, mention, libation, vacation, vocation, location, exhalation, installation, implication, flagellation, appellation, revelation, education, &c.; 6thly, with ch, as chicanery, seneschal.

In many words is a superfluous t, as in hitch, ditch, pitch, witch, switch, stitch, flitch, stretch, sketch, etch, fetch, wretch, notch, botch, hotch, potch, watch, latch, match, batch, catch, hatch, patch, hutch.

In some words is a superfluous d, as badge, ledge, sledge.

And a superfluous k is very common.

Some of the above substitutions are perhaps natural enough, in consequence of the fact of extra sounds, having no special characters for them in the alphabet, which was phonography for the Latin language only. But there are the same perplexing changes with respect to the regular vowels.

Thus, in the case of e, when it is long, as in fête, — we find it written in five ways, — ay, ai, ea, ey, and simply a.

As 1st, aye, day, bay, fay, gay, hay, pay, may, nay, say, ray, dray, bray, gray, fray, play, pray, array, assay, allay, display, portray, dismay, mislay.

2d. Aid, braid, laid, maid, paid, afraid, staid, bait, gait, wait, bail, fail, hail, jail, mail, nail, pail, quail, rail, sail, tail, wail, frail, flail, snail, trail, avail, entail, assail, fain, gain, lain, main, pain, rain, vain, wain, train, grain, brain, stain, sprain, swain, drain, dainty, portrait, saint, faint, paint, quaint, plaint, aim, claim, maim, tailor, jailer, traitor, sailor, raiment, caitiff, plaintiff, prevail, contain, chilblain, sustain, upbraid, declaim, exclaim, proclaim.

3d. Break, steak, great.

4thly. They, convey, survey, &c.

5thly. Any, many, legation, asparagus, virago, volcano, verbatim, arcanum, potato, octavo, tornado, and words ending in ace, ade, afe, age, ake, ale, ame, ane, ape, ase, ate, athe, ave, ary, aste, aze, base, case, face, grace, lace, mace, pace, ace, bade, fade, shade, made, wade, safe, chafe, cage, sage, rage, gage, stage, page, wage, plumage, foliage, cottage, bake, cake, lake, make, quake, rake, take, sake, brake, flake, bale, dale, gale, hale, male, pale, sale, tale, whale, vale, bane, cane, fane, lane, mane, pane, sane, wane, vane, bathe, lathe, swathe, cave, gave, lave, nave, pave, rave, drave, grave, shave, stave, crave, ate, bate, fate, date, gate, hate, late, mate, pate, rate, sate, crate, prate, plate, state, skate, slate, waste, baste, haste, paste, chaste, taste, came, blame, dame, fame, frame, game, lame, flame, name, same, tame, frame, shame, cape, gape, nape, rape, grape, drape, crape, blaze, daze, gaze, haze, maze, raze, craze, graze, glaze, honorary, actuary, tributary, sedentary, primary, salutary, solitary, burglary, contrary, &c.

So for the sound of ī long, as in marine, we have sometimes e, sometimes ee, sometimes ea, sometimes ie, as —

1st. — He, she, we, me, mete, glebe, theme, breve, veto, hero, zero, negro, ether, theist, deist, edict, fever, lever, metre, zenith, extreme, supreme, impede, serene, convene, gangrene, austere, cohere, adhere, revere, severe, interfere, persevere, secret, complete, concrete, secrete, obsolete, theorem, torpedo, inherent.

2d. — Fee, bee, lee, glee, flee, free, tree, see, three, eel, feel, keel, reel, peel, wheel, deem, seem, keen, green, queen, teens, ween, deed, feed, heed, meed, need, reed, seed, bleed, creed, leek, meek, sleek, seek, week, cheek, beef, reef, keep, sweep, weep, deep, peep, sleep, beech, speech, leech; spleen, compeer, between, beseech, discreet, steeple, vaneer, career, tureen, moreen, careen, redeem, agreed, settee, razee, degree, agree, decree, grandee, linseed, peevish, esteem, devotee, legatee, referee, repartee, patentee, absentee, privateer, muleteer, overseer, volunteer, chanticleer, domineer, gazetteer, genteel, indiscreet, steelyard, thirteen, &c.

3d. — Pea, tea, yea, flee, plea, bohea; each, beach, breach, bleach, teach, meach, peach; bleak, sneak, streak, speak, squeak, beak, peak, creak, teak, creak, freak, tweak, weak, bead, lead, read, plead, deaf, leaf, sheaf, beam, ream, dream, cream, stream, team, steam, seam, deal, heal, leal, meal, peal, seal, steal, veal, zeal, bean, dean, lean, mean, wean, yean; heap, cheap, leap, reap; ear, fear, hear, blear, clear, smear, near, spear, rear, drear, year, beard, east, beast, feast, least, yeast, eat, beat, feat, heat, meat, neat, peat, seat, wheat, bleat, cheat, treat, heath, sheathe, breathe, heave, weave, leave, treacle, eagle, eaglet, squeamish, dreary, weary, creature, impeach, anneal, appeal, reveal, endear, appear, arrear, besmear, defeat, release, increase, decrease, beneath, repeat, entreat, retreat, bereave, bequeath, cochineal, eatable, easterly, deanery.

4th. Where the e is silent; either, neither, seizure, surfeit, inveigle, forfeit, mullein, fief, chief, thief, brief, grief, field, shield, wield, yield, fiend, priest, belief, sieve, grieve, belief, achieve, retrieve, relieve, aggrieve, cashier, brigadier, grenadier, cannonier, cavalier, cordelier; also receive, conceive, perceive, deceive, deceit, conceit.

The sound of u is also written oe, o, ew, oo, and ou (silent o), shoe, canoe, woman, chew, brew, screw, threw, shrew, sew, dew, few, jew, mew, new, pew, coo, too, loo, woo, tattoo, bamboo, hindoo, food, good, hood, mood, rood, stood, wood, book, cook, hook, look, nook, rook, took, cool, drool, fool, stool, wool, spool, boom, broom, doom, bloom, groom, loom, gloom, room, boon, spoon, coon, swoon, loon, shalloon, moon, picaroon, noon, soon, poltroon, cocoon, platoon, festoon, monsoon, baboon, coop, droop, hoop, loop, poop, stoop, boör, moor, poor, goose, moose, noose, boot, coot, foot, hoot, loot, moot, root, soot, booty, roof, behoof, aloof, reproof, proof, groove, soothe, smooth, tooth, booth, boost, roost, pantaloon.

It is also written with a silent o, as in tour, croup, group, youth, wound, souvenir, surtout, cartouche, contour, amour, uncouth, accoutre, moustache, tambourine.

I have said that I give to my scholars "Mother Goose," as soon as they have mastered my first "Nursery Reading-Book." But this is for recreation; while all the important *work* is making the groups of exceptional words upon their slates, at my dictation. Sometimes these can be written on the blackboard, and copied into little books, by the children. When there are several ways of writing the same sound, I make several columns, and put at the head of each a word thus: —

i,	e,	ee,	ie,
pin,	me,	see,	grieve;

and then, mentioning different words, ask in which column they are to be put? The children are greatly interested in this exercise; and the effect of it is, to make them know the precise spelling of the words. When a column is finished, they are called on to read the words, and sometimes to repeat the group by heart.

I have not put all the words in the language in my groups; but enough for the purpose, — they can be filled up from the teacher's and children's memories.

The greater the anomaly, the more easily it is remembered, because the specimens are few, and the anomaly amuses.

Thus, I sometimes begin (after I have shown them how to write the extra vowels and consonants, and the diphthongs,) with the word *phthisic;* asking them all to write it on their slates as they think it should be; and then writing it myself, as it is, on the board. So I ask them to write *through,* which they will write *thru.* I then surprise them by writing it on the black-board, and putting in the silent vowel and consonants. Then I ask them to write *bough;* and then *though,* and *dough;* then *trough,* which they will write troth; then laugh, draught, tough, which they will write with f for the gh. In reviewing the lesson the next day, all these words can be written in their manuscript books, with a lead-pencil. The book, which is the best one to follow Mother Goose, and perhaps might precede it, is Mrs. Mann's "Primer of Reading and Drawing." This begins with about twenty pages of words that can be read at once by those who have used the "First Nursery Reading-Book," because the Roman alphabet is a phonography for it all. Mrs. Mann's book is full of sentences that have beautiful meanings, and it contains some attractive stories. It has been out of print a long time; but a new edition is about being put to press.

But any book can be used by a person of judgment. The mother of the Wesleys always taught her children to read in the Bible from the beginning.

In good reading, words are not only to be pronounced, but to be read with expression; and this end is gained by its coming after object-learning. Unless a child conceives what a word means, he cannot have the appropriate emotion, and without the emotion he cannot read with expression. In hurrying children on to read faster than they can understand and feel, permanent bad habits are acquired, and especially the habit of reading without sufficiently filling the lungs with breath; and this not only makes disagreeable reading for the hearer; but is very injurious to the health of the reader.

Dr. H. F. Briggs, of New York, who teaches elocution as a means of health, proposes that there should be exercises of vocalizing, — uttering each vowel sound to express all kinds of emotion which the special vowel will express, and in all quantities and accents. Children are all naturally histrionic and will be amused in doing this. The vowel sounds educate emotions in those who utter them, and awaken them in those who hear. When pronounced with feeling, they come from the chest and abdomen and not from the head merely, and so give a general internal exercise that is healthy. Bronson's "Elocutionist" will give a teacher much assistance in this branch, though he has not worked out the thing so completely as Dr. Briggs has done.

It is proper to remark to those who measure the success of a school by the *rapidity* with which it teaches a child to read, that the thorough attainment of the art here proposed, requires *time*. But when attained, much is gained besides the mere reading, — namely, development of body, mind, and heart.

Besides, to those who are hereafter to be taught other languages it will be found of great advantage to have associated the vowel sounds of ark, ebb, ill, old, and rue, with the characters a, e, i, o, u, respectively. See for the proof of this, some articles on "Kraitsir's Significance of the Alphabet," published in "The North American Review" for 1849.

CHAPTER XII.

GRAMMAR AND LANGUAGES.

Mrs. Mann has suggested, in the last part of this volume, the first exercises in grammar. But grammar is the most abstract of sciences. There are at present few children sent to Kindergartens, who are not too young for the abstracting processes of classing words into parts of speech.

But it is a lesson of orthography, to lead the children to make the few changes which there are in English words, to denote grammatical modifications. For instance, let them write cat, and then say — "If you are talking about more than one cat, what do you say?" They will say *cats*. Let them write at the head of two columns — cat and cats. After some exercises on words adding s only, tell them to write box, and ask, "What if there are more than one?" Then go on and get groups of other irregularities, as changing f into ves, y into ies, &c. Having gone over the nouns, and told all their changes, for number, also letting the children write a list of the nouns that do not change for number, go into verbs, and give the few personal terminations thus: tell the children to write, *I cry*. Then say, "Would you say George cry?" "No," they will reply, "George *cries*." I say, "I have a book; but should I say, George have a book?" They will say, — "No; George has a book." Also by asking questions whose answers shall give the comparison of adjectives, these can be written; and finally the past tense and past participles of irregular verbs. In my own Kindergarten I have given to about half a dozen children who know how to read fluently, and can print very prettily, a little LATIN. It is but a quarter of an hour's lesson, and is conducted in this wise:—Write down *am*. Now, that means love in Latin; but if you want to say he loves you, add *at*, which makes *amat*. Write down *ar*. That means plough; if you want to write *he ploughs* you write what? A bright child said *arat*. Now write down *cant*. That means sing. Now if you want to say he sings, you add what? *at*, then it is *cantat*. But if you want to say *to love* you must add *are* to *am*. They all said *amare*. Now, if you want to say to plough? *arare*; and to sing, *cantare*. Now make the whole sentence, he loves to sing. What is it he loves? They all wrote *amat cantare*. Now write he loves to plough. They wrote *amat arare*. I took the hint from Harkness's edition of "Arnold's First Lessons," and gave them six variations on the four regular conjugations, the infinitive and the third person singular of the present imperfect and future indicative, and Latinized their own names; and they were greatly entertained to improvise sentences, the most complicated of which was, O Helena, Anna loves to dance, Maria loves to sing. I give them no grammatical terms, but only English meanings, and shall not give any cases but the nominative and vocative at present; but I think I shall teach them to vary verbs throughout all the conjugations. It is perfectly easy to give so much of Latin grammar to children in the Kindergarten, because it will not involve the use of a book. They can have a manuscript book into which they can write their words and sentences, in print-letters.

French, so far as it can be taught by merely conversing with the children, is legitimate in the Kindergarten; also any other modern language. But let there be no books used, nor should French be written by the children, for it will confuse their English spelling, and not, like Latin words, aid it. In my Kindergarten, about a quarter of an hour a day is given to making French phrases by all but the smallest children. They have also been greatly interested in learning the French words of a play, which is a useful exercise in pronunciation. I will give the words here:—

L'ESTURGEON (*Sturgeon*).

Commère Perche,
  Je vous salue!
Comment vous portez-vous?

LA PERCHE (*Perch*).

Je me porte très bien, et vous?
  Quelle est l'heure pour le ragoût
Fait de sole et de morue?

LA SOLE ET LA MORUE (*Sole and Cod*).

Commère Perche, je vous salue;
Nous autres ne serons pas un ragoût.

L'ESTURGEON.

  Commère Baleine,
Comment vous portez-vous?

LA BALEINE (*Whale*).

Très bien, et vous?

L'ESTURGEON.

Pouvez-vous sauter en haut
  Comme moi,
Au dessus de l'eau?

LA BALEINE.

  Je ne puis sauter si haut;
Mais je saurais faire jeter de l'eau.

L'ESTURGEON.

Commère Hareng, je vous salue,
Dites moi, je prie, où allez-vous?

LA HARENG (*Herring*).

Je vais chez moi, chercher les jeunes,
Alors nous irons à l'océan.

L'Esturgeon.

Commère Brochet, je vous salue !
Commère Brochet, que mangez-vous ?

Le Brochet (*Pike*).

Je mange des truites
Pour mon déjeuner,
Et des éperlans
Pour mon diner.

L'Esturgeon.

Commère truite,
Je vous salue !
Dites moi, je vous prie,
Qu'avez-vous ?

La Truite (*Trout*).

Ah, par exemple,
J'ai bien grand peur ;
Voilà le brocheton
Même si de bonne heure !

L'Esturgeon.

Commère Requin,
Je vous salue !
Que faites-vous là
Auprès du bateau.

Le Requin (*Shark*).

Je veux manger
Le petit garçon,
Qui pêche dans l'eau.
Pour l'éperlan.

L'Eperlan (*Smelt*).

Petit garçon,
Je vous salue !
Voilà la Requin
Près de moi, et près de vous.
(*Tous les poissons se plongent.*)

The play consists in each fish being represented by a child; and the little boy also. As the Sturgeon asks her questions, she jumps up and down, and as the fishes answer, they jump up and down, till all are in motion. But, before it is played, the whole must be learnt, — which is nearly a winter's work.

CHAPTER XIII.

GEOGRAPHY.

Mr. Sheldon, in his "Elementary Instruction," has shown the way in which we may begin to teach geography without books. To proceed in that way, up to the point of drawing all maps, is feasible in a Kindergarten, if the children stay long enough. My children learn a great deal about the geographical locality of animals, from the natural history lessons given over the blocks. A "Picturesque Geography," compiled by Mrs. Mann, from the most brilliant descriptions of travellers, may by and by be printed, and it would be a good book to read to children. It should be read slowly, requiring them to tell what it makes them see in their fancy. This comprises a great deal of physical geography, and is a desirable precursor of political geography, which will be studied to most advantage by and by, with history. (But history is altogether beyond the Kindergarten.)

Children who have been educated in the Kindergarten thus far, will learn to draw maps. Mr. Sheldon proposes beginning with a map of the room, of the play-ground, and of the town. Guyot's "Map-Drawing Cards," drawn by E. Sandoz, under the direction of Professor Arnold Guyot, and published by Charles Scribner, 124 Grand Street, New York, may here come in play.

CHAPTER XIV.

THE SECRET OF POWER.

In the foregoing pages I have dóne what I can, to make a Kindergarten Guide; not only for the use of those who undertake the new education, but in order to give parents a definite idea of the value of the new education to their children, and how they may aid rather than hinder its legitimate effect. Parents who live in places so isolated as to make a Kindergarten impossible, may also get some hints how to supply the want in some measure, by becoming themselves the playmates of their children.

I think it will be readily inferred, from what I have said, that the secret of power and success is *gradualism.* Any child can learn anything, if time and opportunity is given to go step by step. Then learning becomes as easy and agreeable as eating and drinking. Every degree of knowledge, also, must be practically used as soon as attained. It then becomes a power; makes the child a power in nature; and prepares him, when his spirit shall come into union with the God of Nature, and Father of Human Spirits, to become a power over Nature — "for the glory of God and relief of man's estate."

MORAL CULTURE OF INFANCY.

LETTER I.

My dear Anna, — I had heard of your intention of keeping school before you wrote to me, and had rejoiced for the good cause as only one can do who knows your peculiar qualifications for it. I have been full of the purpose of answering your letter, to tell you how joyfully I look forward to the realization of some of my wishes through your help, such as that of perfecting some beautiful plan of education, which you and I, with our faith in perfectibility, might invent, but which I could not make alone. When we parted many years since, in one of those beautiful porticos of the temple of knowledge, where we had together been warmed by the fires of genius, and where our sympathy (perhaps I should say *yours*) had rekindled a certain torch of enthusiasm that had been long quenched by adversity — (I sadly fear it is smouldering again under the ashes of freshly-buried hope) — I little expected to meet you again in my favorite walk, made fragrant by the breath of little children. If we had chanced to meet often enough since then, we should have found much to reunite us, for my best teachers have been certain wise mothers; — indeed, the only schools in which I have found the instruction I needed, have been the nurseries and firesides to which I have been admitted, often through my loving interest in the little flowers that bloomed around them. I could tell you, if I dared, how many times I have wished I could be queen of such kingdoms, for the sake of the younger subjects of those realms, for I have learned quite as much from the mistakes as from the wisdom I have witnessed.

My desire to gather all I could, from the efforts and experience of others, once tempted me on an exploring expedition through our much vaunted Primary Schools. What

5 *

would you say if I were to tell you that I met with but one spirit kindred to my own in the whole circuit? Among all the hard, knotty women, young and old, whom I found presiding over youthful destinies in this extensive organization, I found one lovely young creature who *loved* all her scholars, and who, by the power of this love, contrived partially to mitigate the horrors of benches without backs, long rote spelling-lessons, crowded and ill-ventilated rooms, tedious periods of idleness in which little darlings had to sit up straight and not speak or fidget (which last I consider one of the prerogatives of childhood). Her face radiated sunshine, her voice was music itself, and yet firm, and she often varied her routine of exercises, prescribed by the primary school committee, with a pleasant little story to illustrate some principle she wished the children to act upon. She was the only one who had interpolated a regular entertaining lesson into the routine, and this she effected by nipping some of the prescribed lessons five minutes each, so as to save twenty for her little treatise upon some interesting subject of natural history. I quite agreed with her that it was a species of petty larceny for which she would be acquitted in the courts above.

I could describe sad, heart-breaking scenes of youthful misery and terror, injustice and daily cruelty in these schools. In several cases my indignation was so much aroused that I was obliged to leave the room to avoid showing my excited feelings. My sympathy for suppressed yawns, limbs suddenly outstretched, or wry faces made behind the teachers' backs; tearful eyes, sleepy little heads nodding on fat shoulders, was so great, that I often smiled upon them when the teacher did not see *me*. I returned to my own little free republic, after spending one of my vacation weeks thus, more resolved than ever not to coerce babes into the paths of knowledge. Many a spine had its first bend there, I doubt not, and many a child learned to hate school in such scenes of discomfort. I have no doubt there were among the teachers many conscientious ones who did as well as they knew how under such a system. If such schools could be presided over by genius, and such geniuses could be left to their own judgment about what to teach and how to teach it, the experience of Mr. Alcott in his first Infant School among the poor of the North End proves that primary Education can be made for all, what we can make it who have the advantage of teaching in our own parlors.

It is astonishing to me that greater improvements have not already been made in this public school education. Often when I am sitting in my pleasant school-room with these favored children of wealthy parents around me, my thoughts recur to those crowded rooms, and the only remedy I see is, that school committees shall be formed of *women*. I believe many of the women I saw teaching in those primary schools would do better if left to their own instincts about the children. They have no liberty whatever, except such stolen liberty as I mentioned in the case of Miss E. What do *men* know about the needs of little children just out of nurseries? If I were one of the school committee, with *carte blanche*, I would have "stir-the-mush" or "puss-in-the-corner" among the exercises, with singing every hour, and marching and clapping of hands. And I would have well-ventilated rooms instead of such hot, suffocating places, warmed by large iron stoves.

And as I see the poor and neglected children in the streets, or in their own wretched houses, and how they live and grovel in low practices, gradually losing the sweet innocence of infantile expression, and becoming coarse and violent, even brutal, I wonder still more at the torpidity of society upon this subject. Nothing is such a proof of its selfishness as this neglect. Nothing makes me feel so keenly the need of a new organization of things. I do not like the thought of merging the sacred family relation in communities where all live together in public as it were, but it seems as if something might be done for the children of the needy that is not yet done. These poor city children are sequestered even from the influences of Nature. How strange that the more favored individuals should not seek every means to give them what culture they can have amid these brick walls. So much might be done by the help of the salient imagination of childhood, that we should be helped more than half way by blessed Nature herself. I often take an unfashionable walk inside the Mall on Sunday afternoon, when the Irish people bring their babes to play upon the green. I think it is the best institution in the city, and it would be a good idea to appoint a Commissioner in each ward to bring all the street children there every day and watch them while they play, and see that all have fair play. If school committees were formed of women, I think such an office might be created.

What faith we need to forgive heaven for the things that are! "How much that is, is *not* right!," I am sometimes tempted to exclaim. I have no idea, however, that Pope meant anything but the eternal IS, when he wrote "Whatever is, is right." It would have been better for superficial thinkers, if he had never said it however, for I often hear it quoted to defend what I consider the marring, not the making of God's plans. I have no doubt there is a remedy for every individual case of misery in this world, if eyes were only open to see it, but this couching process is the needful thing, and *that* God has left us to think out for ourselves. We know that there are millions who live and die in ignorance of all that makes God *God*, or a Father. To these he is only the being that created them, and they may well ask, "Why did he make us? to suffer? to sin?" — for they are conscious only of the irregularities of that creation by which they are tortured. They never see the wonderful adaptation of things to each other; — they know nothing of the harmonies of their being with the being of others, or with Nature. The sort of education they get in cities, where life is stirring briskly around them, and each one seems scrambling to get the best morsel for himself, only makes them worse, unless something is done to evoke order for them out of this chaos. Their belief in Deity is a superstitious feeling about some supernatural power that exercises dominion over them, and subjects them to an imperious necessity. In the agony of death they cry aloud for fear; for they know they have made their fellow-men suffer, and death is a mirror that holds them up to themselves. Conscience breathes upon the glass, and in the dissolving picture its countenance is recognized, — but this is a base fear, and cannot be called an aspiration. To make sure the foundations of faith in God, one must know what God has done for him. Man must be made acquainted with his own nature before God's benevolence can be realized. If I did not think ignorance was at the root of all human evil, I should not have any hope; but though its kingdom is very large, no despot can be so easily driven from the throne. I hope all this does not seem irrelevant to the matter we are discussing; it brings me nearer to the point I wished to reach. I believe in that redemption which knowledge and principle combined bring to the soul that has slumbered in darkness. Its recuperative power is its most glorious attribute. The tendency of the character is so often imparted in earliest youth, that if this is right, if the first impressions of life and its author are the true ones, the rest of the education may almost with impunity be left to what is called chance. But if a child lives to the age of eight or ten years, without a ray of light which will explain his existence and position to himself; or lead him through Nature up to God; it must be difficult to inspire him afterwards with the true filial feeling toward his heavenly parent. And if, by a longer period of darkness, he has found that in a certain sense he can live without God in the world, he will stand a poor chance of realizing that he cannot do so in ordinary life after the period of impressible youth is past. I believe the soul will to all eternity have renewed chances to redeem itself; but I cannot easily give up this first life. When I think of the beautiful adaptations of the world to our wants; of the exquisite gratification the knowledge of there brings to the mind; of the harmonies of our existence with all other existences; and of the power of virtue to triumph over the earthward tendencies of this double human nature, and to sacrifice the present to the future good; — when I think of what the perfect man can be, — I cannot be reconciled that *one* should live and not have the keys to unlock this part of the universe. Childhood is in our power. The helpless little beings must be taken care of. The world waits upon the babe, as has truly been said; and is not this one of those beautiful provisions of Nature which show us how

> "There's a divinity that shapes our ends,
> Rough-hew them as we will!"

"The child is father of the man," indeed; and while the heart bounds lightly, let us teach this youthful father the religion of Nature, which he can understand. When he comes to riper years he will be ready to comprehend the religion of the Spirit, without danger of superstition or bigotry.

One obstacle to such instruction in Christendom is, doubtless, the very prevalent feeling that the study of Nature leads to scepticism about revealed religion. This injury has been done to religion's self by the fact that a few learned men have been scoffers at Christianity, or rather at what has been accepted as Christianity, and it is the association of their names which is the foundation of the prejudice. The discrepancy also between the discoveries of science and the imagery of the Hebrew poets who *sang* about creation, is another cause; but since Mr. Silliman has ventured to say that there probably were a great many deluges, the ice of that difficulty has been cracked in *our* community.

I see no reason why simple religious lessons, like those Mr. Waterston gives in his Sunday-school, may not be given in the public schools. You will say, we must have Mr. Waterston to do it, (and that is true indeed, now,) but when the public mind is ready for such instruction, such teachers will come up to supply the demand.

My first introduction to natural science was in listening to instruction of this kind given to children older than myself, under the sanction of a mother's authority. They were lessons in Astronomy and Chemistry, given before there were any elementary books upon such subjects; and they so kindled my imagination, when a very young child, and gave me such a realizing sense of the presence of God around me, whom I had already known as a Heavenly Father, who took care of me and of all men, by night as well as by day, that from that time I never lost the child's sense of nearness, or felt any of those fears of the supernatural which haunt the imagination of uninstructed childhood. And yet I was in the habit of listening to the stories of an old crone who believed in the witches of Salem, where she had always resided, as firmly as she believed in the God that made her. When I first heard the remark that the study of Nature tended to make men atheistic, I resented it with indignation, though but a child.

This, then, is the kind of teaching that I think adapted to childhood. It need not be exclusive, but let it predominate. Other faculties, beside the emotions of wonder and veneration, may be cultivated side by side with these. Memory, comparison, judgment, and calculation may be strengthened by a judicious and well-proportioned teaching of the elements of languages and numbers, thus insuring the tools for future acquisition. But this is not direct food for the soul. The young heart is full of love for its parents, of delight at the knowledge of new things, and these affections may be guided into adoration of Supreme Intelligence; this love of knowledge turned to its source, as easily and naturally as the stream flows from the mountain to the sea.

Side by side with this higher cultivation I would teach the eye, the hand, and the ear to practise, and to work readily. The pencil should ever be in the hand, the picture before the eye, — especially when the objects of Nature cannot be, and sweet sounds in the ear. The love of activity is sufficient aid without the debasing influence of emulation. Facts are divine teaching, and a clear perception of them the basis of all theories; therefore they should be clearly and sharply presented and discriminated. When children are led to see their own ignorance, let them understand that we, who appear to them the concentration of all wisdom, ("Pallas-Minervas," as one of my little readers of Homer called me one day), are also ignorant in presence of the universe, which is full of things to be known, and they will not be discouraged, but only more eager to learn what they can of these worlds of knowledge; and will think of those still to be conquered rather than of any little acquirements of their own, thus escaping the dangers both of despondency and vanity. Let children lead this happy life till they are eight or nine, and let it be so full and blessed by love, sympathy, and the play of the creative imagination, that it will lift them over the rough places for many more years, while they shall build stone walls and towers of facts, as starting-places for future flights. It is the observation of every experienced heart that the most hardened sinner may be more easily redeemed, if he can be reminded of an infancy of purity and golden sunshine. If true, it is an argument for prolonging that infancy as far as possible, that the recollection of it, if unfortunately dimmed, may the more surely revive in those deep moments of existence, when the soul is thrown back upon itself for support and consolation; whether they be moments of guilt or of sorrow, of disappointed ambition or disappointed hope, of wounded pride, or wounded faith.

I am aware that the public schools are the hope of our land and its glory, and schools are the best world for children to grow up in when properly regulated; but I wish they need not be so large, so that there need be but one sovereign in each. Still more desirable is it, however, that none but living souls should ever have the privilege of unlocking the treasures of knowledge and thought for children. It is not enough to have deep and varied acquirements, but there must be a native delight in communicating, and a sympathy — a living sympathy — with every human being. These alone will awaken the love of excellence and call forth the powers of the mind. No one should ever have the care of children who does not love them because they *are* children, or who can ever feel the undertaking an irksome task. I always regret to see the occupation entered upon as a last resort for a livelihood, or by those whose spirits can no longer respond to the touch of childhood. It must be a strong spirit that, in such instances, can rise again to meet the bounding hopes of fresh being. It is like going back to principles, when our experience fails to answer our just demands for highest happiness. In the faith of childhood, which knows no doubt, we can see that one experience is not the test of what our birthright is; and while we do not neglect the warnings we have had, we must never think that our single experience has exhausted the source whence truth flows.

I believe, too, that the germ of everything is in the human soul; and this faith seems to me essential to a teacher. Education is not the creation, but only the bringing forth of these germs, and that alone is a true education which brings them forth in fair proportions. To make children learn something tangible, if I may so speak, and to keep them quiet, are the usual aims of a teacher, and success in these is the usual test of his value; but they seem to me not to be his highest merit. I have often waited long, and I have learned to wait patiently, for anything like *results*. There is a certain harmonious play of the faculties, to the production of which I direct my efforts, and which I watch for with intense interest in my children, (for they seem to me mine,) and this can never be cultivated if one is bound by any formulas. I consider myself fortunate that my own mind has always enjoyed its birthright of freedom; that no iron habits have bound me to any mechanical system. My advantage is a negative one, perhaps, for I never had much training of an intellectual kind, my physical education being the chief object in my childhood. I was at least saved from such formality as enabled the teacher of a distinguished school to say in my presence, that "the less boys understood or were interested in their lessons, the better the discipline of study." This was surely making the process as mechanical a one as the motions of a trip-hammer. But there you have an immense advantage over me. You have been well trained, and yet measured by no Procrustean bed, for your most living teacher never wore any fetters herself, and could not impose any. Am I not right? Your summer retreat has been "twice blessed" in having such advantages of highest education, added to the influences of Nature, which you so dearly love. You are bound to open your eyes as beamingly as she does, upon all who come under their glance, to show your gratitude for such teachings. I well remember your frequent descriptions of those "large orbs" that presided over the most interesting part of your youthful training. I have seen those eloquent eyes myself, and can conceive their power when animated with the inspiring pleasure of pouring the treasures of thought into a receiving soil. And you are not the only one whom I have heard discourse of this source of inspiration. Your best study, too, was in the season when the reins are generally relaxed. The time when I received most benefit from study, solitary and unaided, and even *stolen* as it was, (for the family decree was that, I being an invalid, must not study,) was when I pursued my lessons in an orchard, and generally in a tree, or sitting in the baby's breakfast-chair, in the midst of a shallow, rushing river, under a sweeping willow. I was brought up so much out of doors, that walls were oppressive to me. Indeed, I look back upon it as the only time of my childhood when any variety of influences acted upon me at once; and one which I ought not to omit to mention, was a much admired friend, who knew how to point out to me, leaf and flower in hand, what riches of knowledge were stored up in Nature for her children. I do not know but what my love of these hidden treasures was stimulated by the fear of being deprived of them. Owing to this fear I probably arrived earlier in life at that point which I have always contended was the great point in education,—the time when one takes it into one's own hands. But I do not think that your "two outward advantages" of motherhood and education, constitute all your qualifications for the task you have undertaken. I know what soil was warmed into fruitfulness by the rays shed from the sun of genius. Now, you are bound to fulfil my hopes, and if my own path is not smoothed by your help, I shall call you to account for my disappointment. I will give you my small experience, and tell you how I found out methods, because they were *not* practised upon me; and I bid forth your power of deducing theories and improvements that will cheer us both onward. For want of more interested auditors, I often pour out my plans for educing order out of the little chaoses committed to my care, to ears that stretch to their utmost for politeness' sake, and for my sake, perhaps; but not for the thing I wish to impart.

LETTER II.

My dear Anna,—I will begin by telling you that I can do the thing better than I can describe it. You must let me tell you stories out of my school-room to illustrate the wisdom of my proceedings. I can hardly tell you my enjoyment of the fresh affections of children, of their love of knowledge (of *new things*, as it always is to them), of their ready apprehension of principles, of their quick response to truth, their activity and buoyancy, their individuality, their promise. Sometimes I look forward for them, and tremble at what awaits them, when I see tendencies to evil or weakness. I know that every ill in their various paths may be made stepping-stones to highest good; but the doubt whether they will be made so, the certainty of the long and sharp pains of conflict, the dying down of hope, (that happily, I know, can yet rise Phœnix-like from its own ashes,) these, and many perils by the way, that my brooding heart points out to me, often oppress me, and I could wish them spared. When it is remembered how man has marred the work of God, how different his part ought to be from what it is, and how long it must be before the individuals of the race can work themselves free from the crust of evil that has grown over the whole, I think I may be pardoned for these heart aches; but I know they are not my highest moments. It has been deeply said that pain is the secret of Nature. I have that within me which responds to it. I must feel it for others as well as for myself, and shall constantly do so when my faith is perfected. I am grateful that I exist, for I can look upon what we call *this life* as only the beginning of a long career, in which I shall ever look back and rejoice that I have been a human being, whatever may be the ills that I suffer from just now. The consciousness of the capacities of expanding intellect and of glorious affections, assure me that the destiny of the soul will compensate for the heritage of woe, which this life is to many of us. Thus I try to look beyond the conflicts I see in the future of these little beings who now dance joyfully around me.

You will wonder, perhaps, that one can conceive such a personal interest in the children of others; but it will come to you in time. You have truly said, that it needs all the tenderness of a mother, and her vital self-forgetting interest in the result, to enable her to find the true path of Nature from the beginning, and remove all obstacles to free unfolding. But many a mother sacrifices her elder children, as it were, to this discovery. As the germ of the maternal sentiment is in all women, relations may be established between teacher and child that may take the place of the natural one, so far as to answer all the purposes required. Such a relation is the only foundation upon which a true education can go on. It leaves no room for a division of interests between child and teacher, which division alone has the power forever to destroy all the best benefits of the communication of mind, and is generally, indeed, an effectual barrier against any *communication* at all. Such a relation as I would have does away with every feeling of reserve that might check the full and free expression of thought and feeling. A young child should turn to its teacher, as well as to its mother, with the undoubting confidence that *there* is a wealth of love equal to all occasions. When my little scholars call me "mother," which they often do from inadvertence, I feel most that I am in the true relation to them. I have in some instances been preferred before the mother, because I was the fountain of knowledge and even of tenderness to starved and neglected little souls. A very sensitive child of seven years old, who always said "can't," when any task, even the simplest, was set before her, but who was, nevertheless, so morbidly conscientious that she was miserable not to be able to accomplish anything that she thought her duty, took an opportunity one day, when she was alone with me, to make me the confidant of her domestic sorrows, asking me to promise I would not tell "mother." This was rather dangerous ground; but I knew something of the domestic life of the family, and that the tender mother of it was often exasperated almost to madness by the cruel tyranny and exactions of the father, and I promised. Then, with burning cheeks and trembling voice she told me that they did not love her at home; that her father despised her; that her mother urged her beyond her strength to meet his requirements; that her eldest sister treated her with harshness and ridicule because she was so "stupid," and that her younger sisters did not like to play with her because she was cross. I saw at a glance why she always said and felt "can't," and I stood awe-struck before the endowment of conscience in the child which had stood the test of such trials as these, and made duty the central point of her being, for that I had already known to be the case. I sympathized with her, as you may well imagine. I told her what I knew of the virtues of her mother, whom she tenderly loved, and whose love for herself she felt, but could not enjoy, because its natural expression was lost in the impatient endeavor to hold her up to her father's unreasonable requisitions. From that hour she was my child, and could work happily in my presence. I told her that I knew she always wished to do right, and that I should always be satisfied with whatever she could accomplish; that if I required too much of her, she only need to say so; that she must not try to do anything more than was pleasant and comfortable, for only thus could she preserve her powers of mind, which were good, and which would work well if they could work happily. Through my influence she passed much time away from her ungenial home, with friends in whose society she could be happy and unrestrained, and the burden was lightened so far that she was in the end able to justify herself, and take a happier place in the family circle; but she was irretrievably injured both mentally and morally, learning to become indifferent where she could not assert herself, and the battle of life will, I fear, ever be a hard one to her.

In such cases one feels the true spirit of adoption, and this should be the standard for the general relation. I do not feel satisfied till the most timid and reserved are confiding to me, smile when they meet my eye, and come to me in the hour of trouble; nor till the most perverse and reckless take my reproofs in sorrow and not in anger, and return to me for sympathy when they are good.

Nor am I willing to have anything to do with the education of a child whose parents I am unable to convince of my vital interest in its welfare, and into whose heart I cannot find an entering place, while at the same time I speak candidly of faults; for there is a sort of magnetism in the coöperation of mother and teacher; and its subtle influence, or the reverse, is distilled into every detail of the relation. Sometimes I find parents who do not know enough of their children to interfere at all, and then I am willing to do what I can to supply the deficiency. The school should only be the larger family for them, and the lessons learned should be the least good they receive from the daily routine. Still worse off are those who are educated at home by servants who rule in nurseries, and so long as they keep the children quiet are not questioned much as to the means by which they do it. Quite aggravated cases of oppression have come under my observation, which I have discovered by noticing the sway held over children by these hirelings, who bring them to and from school. I *think* I should never risk this evil in a family of my own.

To seize every opportunity to unfold thought in a natural way, to consider duty, to awaken and keep alive conscience, and cultivate a mutual confidence and forbearance between the young, should be the aim in such a little world as a school. The flow of happy spirits should be unchecked, and no deep memory of faults should remain with a child, unless they are of the deepest dye, such as falsehood and selfishness. A serious invasion of each other's rights should be made a prominent subject of blame, but the only retribution of which a child should be made to have a permanent consciousness, is that of the injury, or the danger of injury to *itself*, and I firmly believe if this can be made apparent to a child, it may be the strongest possible motive to keep it in the path of rectitude. It seems to me indeed the only legitimate motive to present to a human soul. I do not mean a selfish regard to the welfare even of one's own soul, but that regard which includes the welfare of others as well as of one's own. I do not like to say to a child, "do not so because if you do I cannot love you," for that is an outside motive, but rather "because you cannot grow any better if you do so and then you cannot respect yourself or be worthy of any one's love. "Do not grieve dear mother by doing wrong, for then she cannot be happy." "Are you not afraid if you do so, that by and by you can do something more naughty?" "Is there not something in you, that makes you feel very uncomfortable when you have done wrong? That is the way God has made us, so that we may grow better and not worse." I have arrested *very* naughty doings by such remarks, where defiance of human authority was very strong and determined. I have awakened a similar fear in many a child by relating what a dread I had in my own childhood of growing worse. Nothing is easier than to make a child false by frightening it or blaming it too much; but nothing will make a child so ingenuous as to convince it that you are interested in its progress, and would like to help it cure its own faults. But we must often wait long before a child is capable of taking this view so fully as to be influenced by it, in opposition to the dictates of passion and the weakness or immaturity of intellect; experience teaches us that the volatile, the obstinate, the self-indulgent, the crafty, and even the indolent must be influenced by the apprehension of a nearer penalty or the power of a more direct authority than that can always be understood to be. Self-control is often the first virtue to be cultivated, and a fear of present evil must sometimes be the instrument of its cultivation. A distinguished and most successful superintendent of an insane hospital once assured me, that in the majority of cases, self-control was all that was needed as a remedy for insanity. I asked him if he had ever known of insane children? He said he had known many; and that it usually appeared in the form of *unmanageableness*. If we concede that all evil in our race is partial insanity (and if we believe in the soul, we must finally think that the crust of organization into which it is built for a time is the only obstacle to its right action, and to put one parenthesis within another, which I know is not canonical, does not this point to the duty of providing against evil organizations?), why should we not treat all evil as insanity should be treated, and believe that if the power of self-government is cultivated, the soul will take care of itself? In this connection I always take health into consideration; for one wise mother of my acquaintance suggested a new idea to me by once telling me that for certain faults in her children she always gave medicine, being convinced that the difficulty lay in the stomach.

I am always very careful to disarm all fear before I use any authority. I find much timidity in children, as if they had been harshly dealt with. I have seen fearful looks of terror in little faces when I have approached them to enforce a request, and in such cases I either take them gently in my arms or draw them close to me with a caressing motion, which is sometimes all the punishment they need, if you will allow me such an Irishism. They are at the same time convinced of my earnestness, and disarmed of all opposition, and when I approach another time, if occasion requires, I can lead them to another seat or even out of the room, and enjoin obedience without exciting either fear or opposition. I never threaten any penalties, but execute my own requisitions decidedly at the moment, "because this is the right thing to be done." I think it is not well to threaten for *next time;* and where punishments are mild, such as changing a child's seat, or putting it into a room alone, or going to its mother and talking the matter over in presence of the child, a repetition of the offence may be avoided. I have one child in my school who would crouch down upon the floor, if opposed, or required to do any thing she did not wish to, and go into a sort of hysteric, protesting that she was dying. I laughed at her a little at first, but I soon saw she was very obstinate and very passionate, and several times on such occasions I took her up in my arms, though she was pretty heavy, and carried her to a bed, where I laid her down and left her to enjoy her performance alone. After a while she would sneak down into the school-room again looking very much ashamed, but I took no notice of this, and after two or three experiments she was entirely cured. I learned afterward that she had practised this device successfully upon a doting mother and her nursery-maid, who really feared she would die. They were much

6

obliged to me for having the courage to meet it resolutely. She has become a charming little scholar, for she is as full of talent and affection as of self-will, and has been sent, by my urgent entreaty, to learn calisthenic exercises, where she expends the extra fluid which, when bottled up by inaction, works mischief in her. She was formerly unable to tie her own bonnet or draw on her own gloves, but in six months she has so changed that she can dress other children as well as herself, and climbs the banisters and perches herself fearlessly upon the tops of the doors, greatly to the terror of other little children of luxury like herself.

We should never prevaricate or in any way deceive a child for the sake of an immediate result, for that is not being true to principle, but we may be allowed sometimes, in our characters of mothers and teachers, to act as that "near Providence," which the mother has so happily been said to be. In God's government, some penalty, though often a hidden one, is the consequence of every transgression of law; and do we not in a small measure act to the child as his representatives? It is a dangerous power to have dominion over another soul, even for a time; but since it is actually given to us, are we not bound to make use of it, conscientiously and tenderly, but still to make use of it? I once knew a father who thought, because he was not himself perfect, that he had no right to exact obedience from his children. His retribution for this morbid conscientiousness was most deplorable. One child became insane from want of self-control, which he would not allow her to be taught; and another failed to have any sentiment of duty toward God or man, but passed many years of life without apparently knowing that any duty was required of him. Worldly prosperity in his case only increased the evil, for he was never obliged to make an exertion for himself or others. I have never heard that he was vicious, but he could not live even with the parent who had allowed him to grow up unrestrained. The parents surely are designed to represent to the child the Heavenly Father whom they cannot see, and who must later become an object of faith through that beautiful analogy of parental love and care.

I agree too with one of the best and wisest, who has said that it is not necessary to reward children for doing right, since God has so made man that doing right is, like loving, its own reward. Only those who have thought deeply can make such discriminations as these, yet to what noble mind, when the thing is once said, does it not seem base to give an outward reward for a lofty action? And is it not a brotherly act to help our fellow-pilgrims on their way, by giving a friendly warning when a stumbling-block is in the path? I think children can be made to understand that a judicious punishment is a friendly warning, if not the first time we administer it, then the second, or the third, or even the fiftieth time; for as we should forgive, so we should warn our brother, "not seven times, but seventy times seven." I learn to feel that if I am actuated by the right motive in my dealings with their souls, (and one learns to be very conscientious in meddling with them,) my pupils will find it out sooner or later; and then they will see all that I have done, as well as all that I may do, in a new light.

I have a bright little fellow in my school who had acquired a sad habit of sucking his thumb. I thought he actually began to grow thin upon it. I had checked him many times, and he was good about it, but the habit was too strong for him. One day I drew on a little conversation about helping each other out of difficulties, which all agreed to; and all professed themselves willing to be helped and to listen to warnings. I then said there was one in the school whom I wished to cure of a bad habit, and I had a plan for doing it, but its success must depend upon whether he was willing, and upon whether the rest would be really friendly and not laugh at him, or tease him, but help him in every way they could. They were very desirous to know who and what it was, and very sure they would do all that was desired. I then spoke to little W——, who was only six, or at most, seven years old, and asked him if he was willing to let me tie that hand behind him that he might be cured of sucking his thumb; for I knew of no other way. I told him it would try his patience; for it was his right hand, and he would have to be dependent upon others for many things, and often would find it very inconvenient and annoying. After I had impressed him fully with the importance of the matter, he consented, and the rest of the children promised to be attentive to his wants. I never tied the hand behind him till he put the thumb into his mouth; but it had to be done every day for a fortnight. He bore it, and all the inconveniences, like a hero, and not one child forgot to be considerate and helpful. He was cured of the trick, and he has been an object of great interest among his companions ever since, because they helped to do him good.

Perhaps, dear A——, you will think I dwell longer than necessary upon this subject, knowing as *we* do that the usual fault of schools is too much penalty, and too much low motive; but you and I are surrounded by those who are inclined, by their tendency of thought, to forget practical wisdom; who, in their lively sense that immortality begins now, and is not a distant good, — a sort of reward for well-doing, are in danger of forgetting that we are to be educated by circumstances, and that circumstances *will* educate us, whether we direct them or not, in this beginning of our long career. Those who have most faith in the soul and its ultimate power to work itself free from all impediments, are most apt to despise all the minor aids that may help its first steps.

Then there is another class of persons, who do not believe in the soul enough to think education of any use. They cannot very well tell you what they do believe; in truth they have no faith in anything, but finding it hard to control circumstances, and seeing instances of great failure where there have been most appliances, (they do not consider whether these appliances were wisely administered,) they give all up to chance, and believing neither in innate ideas nor in the use of means, rest satisfied with a low standard of action, and go through life without ever having a glimpse of anything better than themselves. Indeed, if they see anything better, they understand it so little, that they think it must be a delusive appearance, and that an earnest view of any subject is extravagance, or even insanity. But I do not think so great a want of faith is very common.

This is too long a letter, so good-by for the present. When I think you are rested from this, I will write again.

M.

LETTER III.

My dear Anna, — Let me introduce you to my little family. It consists of twenty children, some of whom have been under my care for three years. These latter are eight in number, and from nine to twelve years of age; then I have six who are not seven years old, who know how to read pretty well, but who study no lessons more difficult than a simple bit of poetry, the names of a few places on the map, a list of words from the black-board of the parts of a flower, or an interlined Latin fable, which I give them thus early, because Latin is one of the elements of our language, and its forms are so definite that it gives definiteness to ideas. These children print, write, draw from outlined forms and blocks, as well as from their own fancies, and listen to all sorts of information which I give them orally, and which they recount to me again when questioned. I tell a great many stories over maps, which are, in my dominions, not only lines running hither and thither with a few names interspersed, but real mountains, rivers, lakes, and seas, which I clothe with verdure, and people with all kinds of animate forms, such as beasts, birds, fishes, and William Tells, or other interesting individuals and tribes. I have a book, called "Wonders of the World," which is my Aladdin's lamp, and when I take it down, little hands are clapped and bright eyes glisten.

But I must not forget to mention my other six, who are sweet little buds of promise as one can well imagine; who love to hear stories about all living things, from oysters up through the more intelligent shell-fish that have heads as well as a foot, to small pink pigs and their mothers, butterflies, birds, dogs, horses, cows, and fellow-children; and to learn that their stockings are made of wool that grew on the back of a lamb, their shoes of the skin of a calf, their ribbons from the cocoons of a moth, the table of a tree, &c., &c. These little people were committed to my keeping directly out of their mothers' or their nurses' arms. I am always diffident about taking the place of the former, but rejoice to rescue babes from the care of the latter.

The first thing to be taught these, is how to live happily with each other; the next, how to use language. It is not necessary to wait till they can read before we begin this last instruction. They love dearly to repeat the words of simple poetry or of poetic prose, (Mrs. Barbauld is my classic for babes,) and it is curious to see how synthetical are their first mental operations, and how difficult they find it to disentangle the words of a short sentence, which evidently has hitherto been but one word of many syllables. Names of things can be made to stand forth distinctly before other words, because the objects of the senses do; but when I first ask children of three or four years old to make sentences and put in *the* and *and*, their pleasure in recognizing the single word is even greater, and they will amuse themselves a great deal with the exercise, running to me to whisper, "just now I said *the*;" or, "Charley said *and*." If the printed word is pointed out at the same time, it is still more interesting, because then it becomes an object of the senses, a real thing, just as much as the book it is printed in. You know I take the royal road to the attainment of this art, and teach *words* first, not letters. I find this a much better as well as happier way, for a word is a whole host of thoughts to a young child, and three words in a row a whole gallery of pictures. Bird, nest, tree! If a child has ever played in a meadow, or even in a garden, or sat on a grassy bank under the window, or has seen pigeons fly down into a city street, what subject of endless conversation does this combination of things present! The book that contains such words, and perhaps a story, of which they form a part, is itself an illuminated volume, and is immediately invested with a charm it cannot lose, for what child (or man) was ever tired of the thought of a bird, or a tree, to say nothing of that more rare and mysterious object, a nest? The warbled song, the downy breast, the sheltering wing, the snug retreat, have such an analogy with the mother's carol or lullaby, the brooding bosom, and the beloved arms, a child's dearest home, that every sentiment is enlisted, and a thousand things, never to be forgotten, may be said. There is no need of pictures on such a page as this. I well remember the shining pages of my childhood's books,—a lustre never emitted by white paper alone. I doubt not the ancient fancy of illuminating the works of great minds with gilded and scarlet letters grew out of some such early association with printed, or rather written thoughts; — for printing was not known then.

I believe you do not approve of this method of teaching to read; but I cannot help thinking a variety of experience like mine would make you a convert to my mode. I claim to have discovered it, and the bright little six years old rogue, upon whom I tried my first experiment, learned to read in six weeks, and every word was an experience to him, for I made up the lessons as we went on from day to day right out of his little life. He would scream with delight to see what he called *his* words on the sheet upon which I daily printed a new lesson. I have no doubt every name of a thing looked to him like the thing itself, for his imagination was a very transmuting one. You would have been as amused at his antics over the word "and" as I was. I only introduced such oysters of words occasionally into my gallery of pictures, but he never forgot any such useful members of society, though I think he could not have made pictures of them. One great point is, that children are always happy to read in this way; and to work their little brains against their will, seems to me cruel. It is quite an effort for them to learn to observe closely enough to distinguish such small particulars even as words, with which they have such vivid associations, and altogether an unnatural one to learn arbitrary signs, to which nothing already known *can* be attached. Until I was convinced that this was the best method, I always found myself instinctively helping innocent children along, through their first steps in reading, by means which, at the time, I half thought were tricks, and unsafe indulgences. I feared that I was depriving them of some desirable and wholesome discipline, such as we often hear of in our extreme youth from nursery-maids, who tell stories of parents who whip their children every morning that they may be good all day. But I will never again force helpless little ones, of three or four years old, to learn the alphabet and the abs, until every letter is interesting to them from the position it holds in some symbolic word.

When letters are learned in the ordinary way, they are often associated with some image, as *a* stands for *apple*, *b* for *boy*, *c* for *cat;* and these associations may be so many hindrances (certainly in the case of the vowels) to the next step in the process, because they must all be unlearned before the letters can be applied to other words. In our language there are so many silent letters in words, so many sounds for each vowel, and the alphabetic sound of the consonants is so different from their sound in words, that I do not care how late the analysis is put off.

After a while, I string columns of little words together, in which the vowel has the same sound, as *can*, *man*, *pan*, *tan*, and let these be the first spelling-lessons; but I prefer, even to this mode, that of letting children write from dictation the words they are familiar with on a page. One dear little boy came to school three months before he wished to read, or to look at a book, except for the pictures. At last he came into the class without an invitation, and has learned very fast, and can read better than some children who have read longer. He is a perfect little dumpling, as gay and happy as a lark all day, and I would not for the world make it a task for him to use his brain, thus risking the diminution of his rotundity. He is as wise as a judge, though he has not lost his baby looks; and he might be made to reason subtly at an early age I doubt not; but I hope all such powers will be allowed to slumber peacefully as yet. He is in the mean time learning to read slowly; to print, to draw houses, to repeat poetry, to sing songs about birds, bees, and lambs, and to have as much fun between these exercises as I can furnish him with, — the latter in another apartment, of course. I have taken no pains to teach him his letters. I have a great repugnance to *letters*, with their many different sounds, so puzzling to the brain; — but one day, finding he knew some of them, I pointed to *g*, and asked him if he knew the name of it. He said "grass," which was the first word in which he had seen *g*. So *w* he first called "water," for the same reason. I gave him their sounds, but not their alphabetical names. I was obliged to give him two sounds for *g*, one hard, one soft, and he soon knew all the consonants by their powers. I hope he will not ask me anything about the vowels at present.*

* All these difficulties with which I wrestled so many years in my character of *champion of childhood*, are entirely solved and done away with by the more recently introduced method, — introduced by authority of a distinguished philologist, of teaching the Italian alphabet, and always calling *c* and *g* hard, as the old Romans are supposed to have done. This mode is made practicable in the "First Nursery Reading-Book," and the last edition of the "Primer of Reading and Drawing." Abundant experience shows that reading taught in this way leaves nothing to be unlearned in English,

I also cut out the words children first learn, as soon as they can put together a few in short sentences, and let them arrange them to correspond with the sentences in the book. I have devoted one copy of my Primer to this purpose, and keep the words thus separated, and pasted upon card-board, for such use.

I know all children learn to read, and some children learn rapidly, but I am always interested to know at what cost. It is a very important question, I assure you. One may not realize, at the time, the evils consequent upon the difficulties first encountered. The actual injury to the brain stands first among these. We grown people know the painful sensation consequent upon too long and too fixed attention to one subject, even in the arranging of piles of pamphlets which we are endeavoring to classify. The brain whirls and experiences chills, and the whole body feels it. So with children, when made to read too long, before the eye has learned to discriminate words easily. The child is told that it is naughty, if it does not continue as long as the teacher's or the mother's patience holds out (as soon as that is exhausted, the lesson is sure to be over). How false this is! A little child should never be required to do anything intellectual as a duty. It should not be required even to *love* as a duty, much less to think. Both should be made inevitable by the interest inspired; its mental efforts should only be sports. Its habits of self-control, its kindness, its affection, should be cultivated, and this rather by example than by precept. When mothers do not succeed in teaching their children to read, because they have not the resolution to force them to it, they often say to me, "Do teach the child to read, it will be a great resource;" I reply, if I think they will be-

and teaches an analysis of words into letters which contributes very much to the ease of the subsequent study of European languages, to which the sounds of the letters of the Italian alphabet apply almost without an exception. Experience upon this subject has given me confidence in the general rule of *never* teaching exceptions to anything until the rule is well understood and mastered.

lieve me, that their instincts have perhaps been wiser than their understanding; but if I see that they are unreasonable, I reply that I will try, reserving to myself the privilege of trying just as much as I please, and no more. I can generally make the effort to read a voluntary one, if I do not find any previous painful associations to do away. If I do, I wait patiently till I can replace them by others, and in the mean time make books vocal of such enchanting things that the desire will bubble up in the little mind, through all the rubbish that has gathered over it. The pleasure of reading together from a black-board, on which the letters should be printed with great exactness and perfection of form, in order to resemble those in the book, often gives this desire.

One little fellow, whose perceptive powers are sharper than those of my dumpling, reflects upon himself more, and although equally fat, appears, from a certain anxious expression on his face, to have had some trials. He says his sister sometimes "hurts his feelings." He thinks some words are beautiful and "full of pictures." He tells very small fibs, such as "Mother says I must read those words, and those." Do not suppose I let this fibbing pass. I make a great point of not believing it, and of comparing it with truth, and of proving to him that his mother knows nothing about it.

Another little darling, who cannot speak plain, says, "Oh, is 'at *feathers?* Why! is it *feathers?* Oh, now tell me where *wings* is! Oh! is 'at *wings?* Oh! I want to kiss oo."

I hear these little ones read four or five times a day. The lesson occupies about fifteen minutes each time. All "study" together, as they call it. I put my pointer on the book of each in turn, making it a habit that they shall not look off the book for the space of three minutes, perhaps, during which each reads. They keep within a few sentences of each other, near enough to think they read together, as I detain them long upon the repetition of all they know; but I see very clearly which will start off soon and outstrip the rest. I say nothing of which reads the best, but sometimes make such remarks as, "L—— will learn to read very fast, I think, he is so attentive." This makes L—— all the more attentive, and helps the others to make the effort; for with these four, to be able to read is the most charming of prospects. I am determined that no touch of weariness shall break the charm. In three months they will be able to read the two first stories in the Primer, which occupy about two pages. Their eyes will by that time become so accustomed to analyzing the looks of the words, that they will be able to print them without the book, and soon new words will be learned very rapidly. I stave off the spelling as long as possible, but you may be sure that these children will spell well by and by. I am convinced of this by experience, for the next class above these in age have begun within a few weeks to write stories of their own, composing instead of copying them from books, as they have done for two years, and I am myself quite astonished at their spelling. They have never spelled a word they did not understand, and their spelling in composition is better than that of some children still older who learned to spell elsewhere, and who hate spelling-books.

One of my exercises in thinking is to ask the children to tell me the names of all the actions they can think of; and to help them I say, for instance, "What can the bird do?" "What can the fly do?" "How many things can the fly do?" Another is to ask them what things are made of, and where they are found, "Are they vegetables, or are they from animals, or are they minerals?" They are vastly entertained by this, and one little fellow became so much excited, and wearied himself so much with his investigations at home, that his mother begged me to suspend the exercise for a time. Jemmy's head is a little too big for his body; and the look of research in his great eyes gives evidence of precocity, the thing of all others to be shunned. His mother has put thick boots upon him lately, and turned him out into the snow, and he looks like a butterfly in boots, with his ethereal head and spiritual orbs.

I have but one child under my care that I call a prodigy; and my influence has not yet been strong enough to check her ardor as it ought to be checked. She is sent to school because she is happier at school than in the nursery, to which rich people's children are so often banished. (I never intend to have a nursery in my house.) This child has been with me three years, and is but six now. She might be made one of those wonders of learning that occasionally astonish the world, if the plan of her education had not been to supply as little food as possible for her cravings. Fortunately she did not ask to read for a long time, but I have not a scholar so perseveringly industrious, so absorbed in whatever she is doing, so full of nervous energy. She is as conscientious as she is intellectual. I have never had to repeat a request to her, or to subject her to a rule. She always sees and does the fitting and the lovely thing. Before she learned to read she would sit for the hour together with a book in hand, (upside down, perhaps,) and improvisate stories wonderful to hear, in which the characters preserved their individuality, and the descriptions of nature were as vivid as those of a poet of many years. She was quite lost to outward things while improvisating thus. One day after school, the maid who came for her not having arrived, she threw herself on the floor, and began a story about a naughty child. I cannot now remember all the very words, for it was a year ago; but the qualities of the heroine were a combination of all the faults she knew anything about. If people were ill, she always made a noise; she would shut the door hard if told that it would make people's heads ache. She hid other people's things, and would not tell where she had put them. She was very cross to her little brother, and often hurt the baby. She cut valuable things with the scissors, tore up her books, and left the pieces of paper on the parlor carpet. One day it rained very hard, and her mother told her not to go out, lest she should take cold. She was always disobedient, so she went up-stairs and put on a very nice dress and her best bonnet, with blue ribbons, and thin stockings and shoes, and nothing to keep herself warm, but went out in the rain, and paddled and paddled about, and wet her dress, and spoilt the blue ribbons on her bonnet; and when she came in she was very, very sick indeed, and had a dreadful fever, and people slammed the doors and made a great noise, and she had dreadful, oh, dreadful pains in her head and her side, and she could not eat or drink anything; and at last she died and did not go to heaven!" She stopped, completely out of breath. After a few moments' pause, I said, "Oh, I am sorry for the poor little girl that was punished so much. Was she so very naughty she could not go to heaven?"

She made no reply for some time, and then recommenced in a low, solemn voice: "When she was lying in her bed, she was very sorry she had not obeyed her mother, and a heavenly angel came down out of the heavenly sky and took her up into heaven." After a short pause she burst out again very energetically — "Then how she ramped! She trampled on the clouds, and put her foot in the sun, moon, and stars!" I made no further comment. I rarely interrupted her utterances, for they never were addressed to any one, and seldom indulged in, unless she thought herself alone. They were picturesque and symbolical, but never vague. The moral was always very apparent. But her imagination sometimes clothes objects with a light of its own. I was leading her up-stairs the other day, and as we stepped into the hall, we saw a large spider running before us. She dropped my hand and bounded forward, "Oh, you beautiful, smiling creature!" was her exclamation.

Would not a bird have been her passport into paradise at that moment?

Another of these children was walking in the mall with me one day, when the sun was shining with an afternoon light upon the bare trees, over rather a dreary landscape of snow and ice. "Oh, the trees look like golden twigs," said my little poetess, so full of joy that I could hardly hold her.

This, dear A——, is the

> " time when meadow, grove, and stream,
> The earth and every common sight,
> To us do seem,
> Apparelled in celestial light,
> The glory and the freshness of a dream."

To return a moment to my little prodigy. When she did not for a long time ask to read, she wished to print, and it must have been this practice which gradually so accustomed her eye to the shapes of words, that when she suddenly conceived the desire to read, she remembered them with marvellous rapidity. Everything else was abandoned for the time, and in the course of two or three weeks she could read very well. I had often seen her take up the books which contained the stories she liked, and I supposed, at first, that she must have learned to read them herself in some unaccountable way. She had often repeated such stories from the book from beginning to end, word for word. But I found it was not the case, — that she had never actually read them before. However, I never could trace the steps. Spelling she does not find easy. Even now, several months after she has been able to read currently, if, when she comes to a new word, I propose to her to spell it, she will mention the letters (I never taught her their names, but she doubtless learned them while printing so industriously), and then say again, "What is it?" as if that had not helped her at all. But she never forgets a word after it is once told her. She joins in an exercise I frequently practise with older scholars, of spelling a few lines of the reading lesson, but she is not so ready as the others, although none read better, and few as well. She now composes stories on the slate instead of improvisating aloud so much; and I am surprised to find how many words she spells aright. But I try no experiments upon her, as my plan is to clip her wings.

If she was enshrined in as rotund a body as some of the other children, I might venture a little, but she already looks too ethereal; — one sees at a glance that the sword of her fervent little spirit might easily be made to cut its sheath.

Children love to use their fingers, and I give them a slate when they come to school, and teach them to print, which accelerates the learning to read. I encourage them also to draw from beautiful outlines, from things they see in the room, and also from their own fancies. I draw upon the black-board before them, very slowly, giving directions for imitation. I never criticise their productions, whether successful or not. I often see a promise in the freedom of a stroke, or in the child's appreciation of his own drawing, which an unpractised eye could scarcely detect. If a little child brings me a slate with three marks drawn upon it which he calls a horse, or a dog, can I be so unsympathizing as to question it? Perhaps I add ears, legs or a tail, and my little disciple does not know the next moment whether he or I completed the picture, but the next specimen of his art will probably have at least one of these appendages.

I drew on the black-board to-day, a square house, with a door in the middle of the front, a window on each side the door, and one in each chamber over the parlors. Two chimneys surmounted the house, and the windows were divided each into six panes of glass. These things I mentioned as I drew them. It was not many minutes before I was called to look at two houses of four times the size of mine, with the additional embellishments of stairs to go up into the chambers, one of the windows open (which I thought decidedly the stroke of genius in this artist), smoke from the chimneys, steps to the doors (my house had been left hanging in mid-air), pumps with individuals, I cannot call them men, suspended to their handles, and various other hieroglyphics which I could not stay to hear explained. These limners are four years old, their faith in themselves and others yet unshaken, and I should be the last one to suggest that stairs could not be seen through the walls of a house, or that men were not lines and dots, or birds as large as houses, for I have known children to cry at such criticisms, and to be quite checked in their artistic exploits by a laugh.

After such rude practice as this, the child, by imperceptible advances, begins at last to see things more as they are, and then a little criticism is safe, but it must still be guarded, sympathizing, and helpful. The next thing to be inculcated after this is that objects must *not* be drawn just as they are, but only as they appear. I made this remark to a child of seven to-day for the first time. He had learned too much to make similar mistakes to those of the little people lately mentioned, but in attempting to copy the drawing of a stool, he could not comprehend how the rungs that joined the legs of the stool could be drawn so as to look right, because one of them could not *really* be made to pass behind the leg. I pointed to a chair and told him to suppose he was drawing it upon the wall near which it stood, for his paper represented that wall, though for convenience sake it was laid flat upon the table. I asked him if he could see the whole of the legs farthest from him, and if the rungs of those legs did not pass behind the front legs. He saw it clearly. Then I told him we must draw things as they appeared, not as they really were. Nothing must be drawn which cannot be seen, although we know more is there than we can see without going behind it. He was delighted with this discovery. Now he understood about the rungs of the stool, and also why two legs appeared longer than the other two. The stool was finished intelligently, though not with elegance, and the paper was sprinkled with attempts at various chairs which he could see from his seat, some of which really looked as if one could sit down in them, and not as if they were flattened out and hanging against the wall. Some of the legs would have gone through the floor, to be sure, if they had been real chairs, in order to afford a comfortable and even seat, but I saw that the idea was seized, which was quite enough for my unexacting demands. A child much younger and less practised, drew the same stool right, without a word from me, and probably would be completely puzzled were I to give her the same explanation, for art speaks to her without articulate voice. I have one little girl with eyes which she seems scarcely yet to have used. I took a great deal of pains to teach her to draw a little upon the black-board last winter, but if I drew a perpendicular, she thought she imitated me by drawing a horizontal line. I endeavored to wake up the love and perception of form by hanging upon the board various exquisitely shaped vases and leaves, but neither these nor rectangular forms aroused her imitative powers. I never ceased to make these trials, for I remembered that a genius in that line once said to me, "the art of seeing must precede the art of drawing." During the long vacation she resided in the country, and nature must have opened her eyes, for since she came back to school (about two months ago), she has actually been able to imitate quite intelligibly some of those very forms, and prefers some of them to others. I assure you I enjoy her imperfect performances far more than I do the successful efforts of many others. A German friend gave me a book the other day which promises to pour a flood of light upon what I now look upon as my benighted efforts to simplify to children the art of drawing. It is the method of a man of genius, discovered after much groping. He, too, had wooden models made, and stood by them, and pointed out to his pupils which part to draw first, as I have done, but at last he has reduced the whole thing to a few lessons upon some rectilinear blocks, a niche, a cylinder, a grindstone, and a ball. I am revelling in the perfect adaptation I see in it to the end proposed, which is practical teaching of perspective without a word being said about vanishing points, aerial perspective, or any of those technicalities which weary my unmathematical brain, and which I have faithfully administered to myself from time to time.*

* The work referred to, by Peter Schmid, of Berlin, was subsequently translated, and published in the 6th vol. of the *Common-School Journal*,

To vary the occupations of my cherubs, I let them write Foster's prepared copies with a pencil, which helps very much to regulate the motions of the hand, as there is a great interest felt in tracing each mark upon the blue line. They also look at pictures in books and on the wall, where I hang all the pretty things I can find, and tell me what is in them; and sometimes amuse themselves at a table of shells, where I hear them recounting in low voices the histories I have given them of these little tenants of the seas. When I kept caterpillars, or rather raised butterflies, they never were tired of watching the chrysalides, hoping to see the expected butterflies. After these came forth in their glory, we were all poisoned by handling the cocoons, and since that experience of itching hands, and arms, and swollen eyes, I have been afraid to venture upon that branch of natural history. Shells are the most convenient natural objects for children to handle. We talk over flowers often, and I teach the names of their different parts, and encourage the children to make collections of leaves, and learn the names of their shapes, preparatory to learning the art of analyzing them thoroughly. For this purpose I have drawn all the shapes I can find named in botanies, into a book, from which I teach them. Flowers are better for teaching beauty than botany, to little children, as they object particularly to tearing them to pieces.

I have not said one word about my little Robin, who stands most of the time at the window watching the horses in the stable opposite, the scene being often spiritualized by the descent of a flight of pigeons, which he generally apprises us of by a shout. Occasionally he turns round and sits down, and watches inside proceedings, and when an interesting story about living things is in progress, I sometimes find him in my lap, or behind me in the chair I am sitting in. His

and afterwards in a pamphlet called the *Common-School Drawing Master*. It is largely used in the public schools of Germany, and formed a new era in Germany, in the teaching of Perspective Drawing, as truly as *Colburn's First Lessons* formed a new era in the teaching of Mental Arithmetic here.

eyes are blue, and his long golden straight hair hangs down from his tall forehead like a cleft banner of light. Robin will not look inside of a book yet. He is like a caged bird in the city where he is imprisoned in winter. In summer he lives out of doors, and rides on horseback on his father's knee, and holds the reins in driving. His mother says horses are the predominating idea, and also sentiment of his life, at present, and this stable-peep into their city life is duly recounted every day at home. I often mourn over my lost residence by the Common, where the children who looked out of window could see trees and a lovely landscape, but you must not think I allow my scholars to be pent up five hours in the house. Twice a day, I array them all, summer and winter, and take them to our city paradise, which happily is very near. There we actually see a squirrel once in a while. One day we saw a butterfly emerging from its chrysalis, and always the sparkling water and waving trees. And we have clear space and fresh air for half an hour. If you will not tell, I will confess that I have sometimes coasted down the least public side of Fox-hill with a babe in my lap, and I find I have not forgotten how to slide, — an accomplishment in which I excelled in my youth. In wet weather, I put on some of the out-door garments, open a window, and have a merry dance or play. The material for the early cultivation I would give is all nature, and art taken picturesquely. The nomenclatures of science are not for children, but its beauties and wonders are, and may be culled for them by a skilful hand till they have had a peep at the wide range of the universe. I believe you think it best not to open these store-houses until the mind is capable of comprehending them more fully, but I cannot think so, dear Anna. Children's love of nature forbids me to think so. I once opened a little soul's eyes with a bunch of flowers. It was a child who had never been to school before, but who had not been cultivated at home, because her mother had suffered from being over-educated, and wished to try the experiment of *nature*, as she called it, — by which she meant, I perceived, total neglect. She had allowed her, therefore, to grow up in the nursery and in the care of servants, both of which I consider as far from *nature's* teachings as possible.

The child was afraid of me and of the children. She looked at us for about three weeks with a fixed gaze as if we were not living beings, but perhaps walking pictures, her features only occasionally relaxing, I should rather say puckering into a woful wail, which expressed utter desolation and want of comprehension of our natures. She was impervious to all my blandishments, which I lavished more bountifully than usual to meet the case. When spoken to, she answered in a monosyllable, or not at all. When she wanted anything, she spoke one word to convey the idea, as a savage would, (she was five years old), and these utterances were never voluntary. She liked to sit close by her brother, who was two years older than herself, and who treated her with great tenderness and gentleness, though every manifestation from her was of the roughest kind. I was sure, however, that I did not see the whole, for his manner of taking her hand and saying "little sister" was so peculiar, that I did not doubt she was genial to him when not in this purgatory of people.

One day I had a beautiful bunch of flowers from a greenhouse on my table. This child's grandfather owned a greenhouse, but perhaps she had never been allowed to handle the flowers, which were altogether too precious for children, and wild pinks and violets had not been accessible to her. I had been trying many days in vain to interest her about a bee of which I had a picture. I had told her the bee made honey out of flowers. On that day I drew the tumbler that contained these splendid denizens of the greenhouse to the edge of the table, and said, —

"Did you ever see a little bee making honey?"

"No."

"Did you ever go into the country in summer when the grass is all green?"

"No." — (I knew she had.)

"Did you ever see pretty flowers growing?"

"No."

"I will tell you how little bees make honey — did you ever eat any honey?"

"Yes."

"They have a long hair sticking out of their heads, and they put it in there, where that yellow dust is, and there they find a little sweet drop that tastes like sugar, and they carry it home, and put it into a little hole, and then they come and get more, and carry that home, and they put that yellow dust into a little pocket by the side of their little leg, and by and by they get enough to make a great deal of honey."

"Do the bees make it all themselves?" said she, with a brightening look (the first look of intelligence I had seen), and at the same time making a plunge at the flowers.

"Yes," I said, and taking them out of the glass I put them all into her hand, for I did not even know that she could speak plain. She seized them eagerly, and without taking her eyes from them went on volubly asking a great many questions. I described the hive and how they all lived together, and told her God must have taught them how to make honey, for they could not speak or understand anybody's words, and that if they wandered ever so far away from their hive, they always knew the way back again. She held the flowers all the rest of the morning. When school was done, I told her to put them into the glass, and she should have them again in the afternoon. As soon as she returned, she very unceremoniously took possession of them, — the first act of volition she had ever ventured upon in my presence, — and nestling close to me asked me the same questions she had asked before, over and over again, and repeating them, and hearing my answers again and again, whenever she could secure my attention. As long as the flowers lasted, she seized upon them every day, and after they were withered to all other eyes, they retained their charm in hers. I varied the lesson often, by telling her of the silkworm, of the butterflies, and of many varieties of the bee family, and from that time a communication was established between us. She was never afraid of me any more; liked to sit near me; and have my sympathy in all things, provided I did not express it too openly. It was curious to see such *mauvaise honte* in such a tiny thing, for she was always reserved, and often relapsed into long silences, and was wholly without enterprise in matters in which the other children were very active, such as drawing, making block-houses, and even playing. But I could catch her eye at any time by a story of any living thing, and she would sometimes surprise me by the intelligence of her questions. For a long time she could not learn to read, or rather would not. Every new attempt at anything was begun in tears and despair, not from weakness, but from pride apparently. Her mother had begun to think it time to attend to her poor hidden soul a little; and after a long summer vacation which she passed in the country, she came back to school with pleasure and with a new face, and though always backward in comparison with children who had had motherly intercourse, and been taught early to use their faculties, she went steadily on. There was no competition to discourage her, and she learned to read immediately when she once wished to. None but mothers can do justice to little children. She sometimes made me think of your remark that every child needs *four* mothers. But I think the two heaven-appointed parents will do, if they see their duties and fulfil them.

To disarm your opposition about sending such little tots to school, I assure you that many of my mothers tell me that the transition from nursery life to my little community has cured children of fretting and other faults, and that they repeat the occupations of the school-room in their home plays. — Read "Christian Nurture," by Dr. Bushnell.

LETTER IV.

Dear A., — When I have a collection of children around me to whom I am to teach things and morals, I always begin by making a simple statement of the footing on which I wish we shall live together. Prevention is better than cure, and much is gained with children, as with grown men, by expecting from them the best and noblest action.

In a school or in a family, I do not like any government but self-government, yet I wish my scholars to know that I often help the growth of the latter by interposing my authority when that of the inner law fails. When I commenced my present school, I had such a conversation with the children on the first day they were assembled, before there had been time for any overt acts upon a lower principle than the one I wished to inculcate.

My school consists of children belonging to one class in a certain sense of the word, that is, to families of the highest general cultivation amongst us, and what is still more important, to families in which there is a general if not well digested belief in the divinity of human nature. Yet there is a great diversity in the influences upon them. Even among people of the most liberal views there still lurks a sediment of the feeling that there is a principle of evil as well as of good in the human soul, and so people expect their children to be naughty on that ground. Now I do not believe in this. I think all evil is imperfection. It is sometimes very bad imperfection, I allow, and I am sometimes tempted to say poetically, though never literally, that it looks like innate depravity. But I do really believe in individual perfectibility, and that "circumstance, that unspiritual god and miscreator," is our great enemy. Circumstance is a very important personage in my calendar, and a perfect Proteus in the shapes he takes, for he covers not only the common surroundings we call circumstances, but organization itself. Perfection *must* be in the reach of every one by God's original design, and it is only man's marring that hinders its progress, and that temporarily. I hope you have the same instinct about this that I have. I can remember, even when I was not ten years old, hearing some one very severely criticised, who I happened to know had had the worst of moral educations, and I resented the criticism, not because the subject of it was any friend of mine, for it was a person in whom I had no particular interest, but I remember the feeling was a sort of vindication of God's goodness, an *assurance* that he would not judge that unfortunate person harshly or unforgivingly, but that the misfortunes she had brought upon herself, would teach her what her life at home had failed to teach her. How often I have thought of that poor woman in my life!

To go back to my school. I knew many of the families, some intimately enough to know the very peculiarities of the children, others only enough to be able to anticipate the little characters; others were perfect strangers, whom I was yet to study. Many of them had never been to school before, and I knew enough of the usual method of governing schools to be aware that the associations of those who had been in such scenes, were likely to be those of contention for power, the memory of penalties, and a division of interests between teachers and taught. Even at home some of these children had been governed by fixed rules, instead of the instincts of love, and had never been addressed as if they had any sense of right and wrong; others had been weakly indulged, others mostly if not wholly neglected, and left to the care of servants. One little boy and girl, children of wealthy parents, scarcely saw their father from one month's end to another, for he never rose till they went to school; they dined at two and he at five, and before his dinner was done, to which he never returned till the last moment, these little ones were put to bed. Even the elder children who also went to school, saw him only at dinner, for his evenings

7

were usually spent in company, or at some club. I hope this is an extreme case. I should say that the mother in this family was an amiable woman, but not sufficiently like the "near Providence" to counteract the effects of such fatherly neglect.

There was one child, of truly religious and conscientious parents, whose moral influence was null, except indirectly, because they really believed that the human heart was originally depraved, and waited to be saved by special grace from God, irrespective of the conscience; and this girl, who was the oldest of my scholars, had less principle to work upon than any one, and when I first spoke of the cultivation of the mind as a religious duty, she told me very ingenuously that it was the first time she had ever heard such a thought, although she was considered quite remarkable at home for her religious sensibility, and really prayed aloud sometimes like a little seraph, in imitation of her truly devout parents; but she was very untruthful.

A few of the children had been made to feel that every human being has a conscience, which, when enlightened, will guide him right. In these latter the work of growth had already begun, and to them I looked for my allies in the work I was about to undertake. I knew that the best I could do would only come up to the standard that had ever been held up before them.

I seated them all around me and began by telling them how much I loved to keep school for little children, when they were good. But children were not always good, and I was glad to help them cure their little faults before they grew to be great ones, which was the thing most to be feared in the world. I hoped the good children here would help me make the others better, if there were any naughty ones. We must all be patient with naughty people, just as God was. It took naughty people a long time to grow better again. If each child would think about himself a moment, he would remember that he did not always do perfectly right; but God had given everybody a conscience which was sometimes called "the voice of God within us," so every one could improve who would listen to that voice.

There was a right thing to be done in every place. In school it would be necessary for all to keep good order, else it would be impossible to study, where there were so many persons; it was just as necessary too that all should be polite and kind to each other, else there could be no happiness. One unkind person could make all the rest uncomfortable.

After dwelling upon these points till all seemed to recognize their importance, I told them that some people kept order in schools by rigid rules and penalties; for instance, there would be a rule that every scholar who spoke aloud should have a mark for bad conduct, every one that kept order, a mark for good conduct; another rule would be, that every lesson learned well should have a mark of approbation, every lesson learned ill, a mark of disapprobation. The penalties for transgressing rules were floggings, bad reports written for parents to see, keeping lag after school, &c. &c.; the recompense for good marks, either a good report, or a present, — the handsomest prize being given to the one who learned lessons best.

But I did not wish to keep school thus. I had no respect for people who did right only because they feared punishment or hoped for a reward. Such motives made people selfish. I had known of children who would deny having done something they had really done, and try to make a teacher suppose some one else did it; and also of other children who were sorry when some one else got the present. All these things made people selfish, and tempted them to be false. We should do right because it was right, whether it were to bring us pleasure or pain. It was the duty of all to improve their faculties, because God had given them to us for that purpose, and had put us into a beautiful world, and given us parents and teachers to help us prepare for a long existence of which this life is but a small part,—a kind of school in which we are educated for another world.

I wished to have but one rule in my school, and that was the Golden Rule: "do unto others as you wish others to do unto you."

The duty in school was to study well and to keep order, that others might have a chance to study. It would be necessary for them all to respect my arrangements, and obey my wishes for the sake of this order, but they need not think of prizes or marks, for I should give none.

I wished them to govern themselves. This would make it unnecessary for me to watch them all the time. I should soon learn who was worthy of being trusted.

Did they not like to be trusted?

They responded warmly to this.

Did they not like to do as they pleased?

There was, of course, but one answer to this question.

I told them none could be allowed to do that in school except those who pleased to do right, because it was my duty to prevent them from disturbing each other, or from wasting their own time. But I hoped never to be obliged to punish any one for doing wrong. I should make no rules at present, and if I found all were polite, obliging, and industrious, I should never need to make any; but if there were any in school who did not obey conscience, and think about other people's convenience, I should be obliged to make rules for such. I should put the names of such scholars on a paper, and those children must live by my rules, because they had none of their own.

I considered proper manners in school to be quietness, no unnecessary speaking or moving about in study time, politeness to every one, ready obedience to my wishes and arrangements, and industrious habits of study.

I should now leave each one to make rules for himself in his own mind; they might write them down if they pleased. I should like to see what each one would think it right to do in school. They might imagine themselves keeping school, and tell how they should govern it, and what they thought the duties of scholars.

Some of them did this. Their regulations were very strict, their requisitions very great. Those who were then morally ready to apprehend my meaning, have never swerved since from the law laid down at that time.

But it was not long before several names were upon my list. For these I made specific rules, taking especial pains to say that they were not to apply to such or such individuals. If E—— or L—— or S——, for instance, should speak aloud on a pressing occasion, I should not subject them to the penalty, because I knew their principles were good; that they thought of the convenience of others, were studious, &c., &c. I should excuse a particular instance of apparent disorder in them until I had reason to think they were growing careless or thoughtless.

I made the same remark in regard to an occasional want of success in a lesson. I might perhaps have erred in judgment by giving too long a lesson. I might find upon experiment that the mind was not prepared for a particular thing. I should be inclined to think an industrious and conscientious scholar did not feel well, rather than to suppose any want of faithfulness. People must always be judged according to their characters.

I assure you it was a great punishment to have one's name upon my list. These children saw the joys of liberty, and that they could be secured only by doing right. I never saw any system of rewards or punishments have such a stimulating moral or intellectual effect.

Some of my scholars were too young even to be bound in all cases by this law of the general convenience, and these I spoke of as children whose habits were to be formed gradually, and of whom this comprehension of the convenience of others could not always be expected. I called upon the rest to help me keep them as quiet as would be consistent with their good, and took it for granted that none would trouble me by playing or interfering with them. There must, of course, be exceptions to all rules.

There were many occasions of recurring to this conversation, and of repeating its principles. When any overt acts of wrong-doing occurred, when new scholars came, I called them around me to talk about the principles on which we must live and act. These conversations were always interesting to the children, and kept up the government of the school. When I make rules and penalties for my delinquents, I make the rules as simple as possible, and the penalties as nearly like the natural consequences of wrong-doing as is practicable. I never lose an opportunity of inculcating obedience to the inward law as the only sure guide of conduct, and if one's eye is fixed upon this point, a thousand occasions will offer themselves. How can any one who does not believe this inward law to be the only sure guide of conduct govern children morally? I have a friend, quite a distinguished teacher, who believes in original depravity, and that conscience is not an unerring guide, and therefore that religious principle cannot be made to grow out of a child's consciousness, but that it is an arbitrary gift of God; supervened upon the human mind without reference to conscience. He once asked me if there were any religious exercises in my school; if I ever presented religious motives, and what they were. I told him I presented no other, that I made all duty a matter of conscience, and that I never saw a child who did not understand that motive. He said he had no doubt it was the noblest way of treating the child, and brought out the highest morality, but it was not religious education in his opinion! What an admission! the noblest way, bringing out the highest morality, and yet not religious education! His school is the constant scene of religious revivals, and by his own admission the children are told not to keep company with the children of liberal Christians, or of those who go to the theatre! I do not believe in a premature Christianity, so taught as to be able to give an account of itself in early youth.

I once visited an Infant Charity School, composed entirely of children who were not likely to have any kind of instruction at home, so that whatever was taught in the school would be likely to make quite an impression. After a pleasant little exercise in marching and singing, they were seated for a religious lesson. What do you think of the following as a basis of Christian charity? — average age of the children, *eight*.

What are the principles of Christianity?

To love one's neighbor and obey God, to believe in the Bible and the salvation by Christ.

Who are the heathen?

They are people who never heard of the Christian religion, and who cannot have salvation by Christ.

Name the heathen nations?

Indians, Hindoos, the people of Asia, Africa, and the islands in the Pacific Ocean.

What is the difference between Christians and heathen?

Christians serve God, walk humbly, and love their neighbors like themselves. Heathens lie, steal, commit murder, and are full of revenge.

Are all the people in Christendom true Christians?

No, only those who believe that God the Father took the form of man and came down to the earth, preached, suffered, and was crucified on the Cross.

What becomes of all who are not true Christians, and of all the heathen?

They go into everlasting fire.

This was a rote-lesson which the children rattled off glibly.

Modifications of such lessons are given in schools where revivals are considered religious proceedings.

Is it not fearful to think that there is a child in Christendom who is not instructed in the great fundamental truth that God has planted in every human soul a principle of conscience by which it can distinguish evil from good, and which, if obeyed, will *save* it, by some natural process alike applicable to Christian or heathen? The first principle to which a child should be pointed is the principle of law in the human breast. God has so made the human soul that this can be taught to young children if one only knows how to do it. If truly taught, we may safely trust that they can never so judge the much-abused *heathen.*

One day when I was walking in the mall with my little scholars, at recess, some of the children cried out to the others that they must not run upon the banks, or the constable would fine them. The warning was not received in a good spirit, and I perceived that the constable was not in good repute among children. I well remembered the "tidy-man," as our servant called him, of my childish days, and the apprehensions I used to entertain lest he should hook me up with his long pole into the gallery of the church, if I made any noise during service time, and I saw that these children thought it quite desirable to circumvent the constable, and get as many runs upon the banks as could be snatched during his absence.

This was an opportunity not to be lost, and when we returned to the school-room, I asked why they supposed the constable was ordered to let no one run upon the banks.

They were curious to hear a reason. It had not occurred to them, apparently, that there was any other reason than a desire to trouble children. I told them the history of the Boston Common — how much pains had been taken ever since the days of the Pilgrims (whom they know), to keep it inviolate, in order that all the citizens might enjoy its beauties and its advantages; how much money had been expended upon it; how it had been secured as a perpetual possession to all the citizens, and how every attempt to build even very near it, had been resisted for fear of cutting off the fine prospect; that even the cows that used to pasture there, had been turned away that the children of the city might play there undisturbed. I then told them why by-laws were made to preserve the beauty of the banks, particularly just after they were repaired and newly laid down with turf.

When they acknowledged that all this was reasonable, I told them that laws were made for the good of society, and that every *good* citizen would respect such laws. Whoever understood what law meant, that is, whoever knew the law within themselves, would respect the laws of a country or a city that were made for the good of all. I thought my lesson was successful.

One who has not been a great deal alone with the unsophisticated natures of children has little idea how early the highest principles of action can be instilled into them. It does not need many words, as I well remember from the few indelibly written upon my mind by a religious mother, who never comforted my timidity, which was excessive, by anything but principles which my soul responded to: "Do right always, and then you need not be afraid of anything;" and, "Your Heavenly Father will take care of you, and will let nothing happen to you but what is for your good," comprised the religious inculcations of my childhood, varied according to circumstances. And when I first fully realized that Christ, who was held up as a model, was "tempted like as we are," my religious education was complete, except what *practice* could give me. The imagination is as boundless in the images it evokes as imagery itself, and no specific cure for fears of darkness and unmeasured danger can ever meet the difficulty. If a timid child cannot be taught that he is under the eye of a tender and watchful Providence, his childhood may be one long terror, as I have known to be the case. If to this is to be added everlasting woe for wrong-doing, there is no wonder that God must come down from heaven to set things right, and invent a scheme which will virtually annihilate his own original provisions

Many of my children have been religiously educated in the right way, have been made to think of God as their creator, benefactor, and preserver, and the author of all the beauties of nature that they see, and the powers they possess. When I say " we must return good for evil as Christ did, who was the most perfect being that ever lived," they understand me as speaking of a principle which they can apply directly to themselves; for I often add, " Christ said things when he was very young that showed he understood all about right and wrong, and in those years of his life which we are not told anything about in the Bible, he must always have obeyed his conscience, or he never could have preached to others as he did afterwards,"— for the only vital use of Christ's life to others is to make his spirit of action our own, and to believe that we *can* do likewise.

I have been led to think much of this in relation to children, by hearing my orthodox friend talk; for he is a very conscientious man, and his admission that to address the child's conscience was the *noblest* way of treating it, though not the canonical one, let in a world of light upon me touching the unchristian condition of Christendom. How can truth prevail where the noblest appeal is not considered the religious appeal? Truly yours,

M.

LETTER V.

MY DEAR ANNA, — If you wish to know the practical difficulties that arise out of my desire to inculcate self-government, and to keep my own out of sight as much as possible, I will tell you candidly that liberty is sometimes abused in my school; but I have never repented of my principles, and have learned not to be frightened by apparent failures, for I have never known an instance, where I have had an opportunity to observe the result, in which my plan has not answered somewhat to my hopes.

And now I must tell you what are my hopes. They are not to make men and women of children, or to produce perfect consistency of action in youth. They are to put the mind in the right attitude so that the education of life will bring forth the character harmoniously; and to make truth, sincerity, kindly affections, and a conscientious use of the powers of the mind the prevailing characteristics. Sometimes I wait long for the dawning of this hope, but I cannot despair of it as long as I believe in the soul. I do not mean that I think the soul self-existent, independent of God, but I believe it so created that it can right itself at last with due effort to realize His presence in vital laws. To induce it to make this effort is what education is designed to effect, is it not? I have had some children under my care who have come to me deceitful, perverse, without delicacy of sensibility, self-conceited, puffed up with lofty notions of their own importance and that of all who belonged to them; and these characteristics so prominent and offensive that our intercourse was for a long time nothing but war. I had no opportunity to express approbation or sympathy, for the object with them was to defy or circumvent me, and to accomplish their lessons by trickery instead of honest application. These faults were constantly recurring, and I was often strongly tempted to rid myself of the difficulty by declining to keep such scholars in school with others. If my operations had necessarily been confined to one apartment, I should have been obliged to do this sometimes, but in my father's house I had many facilities, and I felt it my duty, if possible, to do what I could for such unfortunate children, as long as I was sure that my influence, and not theirs, prevailed in the school. I saw that vices were made apparent, of whose existence I could have wished innocent children never to know, but I knew it was impossible to sequester them wholly from such contact, and perhaps it had better be under supervision and thus possibly turned to account. Sometimes the beauty of virtue is better seen by being contrasted with its opposite.

Had not I a right to think the evil might be overruled for good, since God permits evil (the negative of good) in his world? To do this, however, requires the greatest vigilance, and occasionally I have been obliged to suspend very much the intellectual training of a school, to gain time to investigate its moral state, and the degree of evil influence that might tend to counteract mine, for these interlopers among the innocents sometimes had bright parts, and an activity that never tired. The faults of such children often brought them into direct collision with their companions whose peace they invaded, and thus far I was aided by my scholars in my discipline, though I have had cases where the outward speciousness was only such as one would imagine to belong to a matured person. I was obliged to take the greatest pains, however, in order not to destroy the very germ of delicacy (which yet bore no fruits), that my admonitions should be in private, whenever no overt acts made it necessary for me to speak before others. In private I need not speak in measured terms.

It is frightful to feel one's self so directly in contact with the wrong-doing of a fellow-being, but at such times I have laid open the heart as well as I was able, and showed the characteristics in all their hideousness, taking it for granted that the moral judgment was still alive.

A great man once said to me that we had no second consciousness by which we could judge ourselves; and Burns, you know, exclaims, —

> "O wad some power the giftie gie us
> To see oursels as ithers see us!"

but I agree neither with the philosopher nor the poet, for conscience is that second consciousness, which can be evoked if only the right conjurer speaks. I believe in no other safeguard than that "voice of God within us" to which I firmly believe no human being is *always* deaf. But, dear A—, what is so revolting as a bad child? It seems an anomaly in nature. I depict no imaginary characters to you. I do not think I could imagine a bad child. It must be seen and known to be believed in. I am always inclined to blame the environment of such a child, but repeated instances that I have known convince me that souls differ in quality, and that it is unreasonable to expect the loveliest type of virtue in all. I believe in the remedial power of education, not that it can change the quality of the soul, but the character of the individual. A bold, free spirit will not by education be made delicate, but its boldness may be employed on worthy objects, and so of other traits. Truth too can be shown to be beautiful to some, but to others to be only manly, or respectable.

I have known children, who apparently had very little sensibility, to be touched by the fact of never being unnecessarily exposed to others. This care awakened in them a perception of delicacy. In one instance, I learned subsequently that reproof received thus in private made a great impression, while that administered at the moment of overt acts of wrong-doing in the presence of the school made very little, or only provoked defiance. I have sometimes had testimonies of affection from such naughty children, and have feared they only proved a want of sensibility, but this instance showed me that my care and painstaking were appreciated where I least thought of it. I have often realized that I kept bad manifestations in check, though the frequent outbreaks of such traits as want of truth, stratagem, attempts at secret influence in the school, proofs of want of delicacy of taste and of conscience, made me feel that all I could do in the short period while my influence lasted, was to hold up my testimony to good principles, and make an adherence to truth, and sincere and conscientious action in every particular of life, — the central points round which all other things must revolve. This I never lose an opportunity of doing by dwelling upon it to others as well as to the guilty. In a small school like mine — yet large enough for variety, — I am in such close personal contact with all my scholars, that the intimacy is nearly as great as in a family; indeed, my personal intercourse with many of the children includes more hours and more actual communication of mind than takes place in some families. It seems to me very important that schools should be of such a size that this may be the case, if they are to be looked to as a means of moral, as well as of intellectual culture; and if they are not, I conceive them to be nurseries of as much evil as good, to say the least. One of the most melancholy things in life, to me, is seeing children get used to what is wrong, submitting to it as a necessity of growth; and a good school, where everything can be talked over, is an immense check upon this. Happily the world cannot spoil a good soul, but there are degrees in goodness, and in moral strength, and even good souls get tarnished by getting used to evil. I would put off the day as long as possible. In cities, where nearly the whole of youth is passed in schools, more regard should be had to the moral part of the training. Knowledge is dangerous power to the unconscientious, and every child should and can be made to feel it.

In such deplorable instances as I have referred to, every power within me has been taxed to the utmost to counteract the evil tendencies that put forth their shoots in every direction. Sometimes a clearness of head that made it easy for a child to see the bearings of things, or even an instinctive affectionateness of disposition (not such as would stand the test of opposition, however), have been the only foundations of my hope. These do not supply the place of tenderness of conscience, but when one is endeavoring to help forward that growth, a clear intellect is an important aid. A natural obtuseness in both departments of the nature would make one's efforts dark and groping indeed.

Now when I thus confess how small has often been the reward for my pains, you may smile at my credulity, but I have had some rewards in the midst of discouragements. I did feel in one instance, before my scholar was taken from me, — and she was taken away because her mother had not the moral courage to let her suffer the natural consequences of her wrong-doing, at a crisis when I felt convinced it might do her radical good, — that she had a far-off glimpse of what character is; that the fine saying of Novalis, "character is a well-educated will," had dawned upon her mind; for she could sometimes tell the truth against her own interest, and could bear the natural consequences of a fault, occasionally, without flying into a passion. My "natural consequences" were, privation from the society of her companions when she had abused their faith and their peace, &c. The child was *willing* herself to sit, for a whole term, in another apartment, and not enter the school-room except for a recitation, and to have no part in the plays of the school, but her mother was not willing.

This child I could not call noble-minded, or generous-hearted, or a lover of truth, or a self-governing being, but I thought she had been able to discern glimpses of these characteristics in others whom she had wronged, and that had given me hope. I was thankful that I had given her principles instead of penalties, and that I had had faith enough to wait for the dawning of light within herself, without giving her up or producing a false shine by addressing lower motives. She would have despised me at that moment, if I had yielded to her mother's wish that I should reinstate her in school before she had outlived her probation, which the child and I had agreed to be the best discipline for her. I am inclined to think she judged her mother unfavorably at that time, for she often came to see me afterward, to ask me if I thought such and such things were right — things which she evidently had heard discussed. She was but eleven, but she had a wonderful power of writing symbolically. She once wrote a legend in imitation of those of Spenser's "Faëry Queene," which showed great intellectual insight into the distinctions between right and wrong, and her sense of her own faults was such that if anything closely resembling them was read of in school, she would put her head under the table, as if she knew and felt its application. The apparent attraction of my society to this child was very significant to me. She would ask me the most subtle questions in morals, and discourse as well as I could, so that I felt as if her knowledge of right and wrong, gained through the intellect, was rather a hinderance than a help to her moral improvement, for she was guilty every day of malicious falsehoods. Her envy of her companions was sickening to the heart, for it made her active in injuring them. She had vanity rather than ambition, for her desire to excel did not spur her to any troublesome efforts, it only made her hate every pursuit in which others excelled her, either by natural gift or by conscientious, patient industry. At such times she would throw her books across the room, and stamp upon the floor like a little maniac. Her unusual brilliancy of imagination, unaccompanied by any sedative qualities, was one explanation of her character. Her wit and fancy gave her great influence over her companions, by whom she was admired, or feared, or held in great aversion. She had a passionate attachment to one girl a little older than herself, who was singularly lovely and delicate in mind and conscience; but this passionate love alternated with fits of persecution, arising wholly out of envy, so that I have known her friend, who was strangely fascinated by her, to be ill for several days, in consequence of painful scenes of its display. This little Italian soul, born under our cold skies, was almost a fiend at eleven years old. Perhaps the intellectual insight she possessed at that early age, will be useful to her at any period of life when her moral nature shall be awakened. I have known instances in which the latter slumbered in childhood, and was roused into vivid action later in life by crushing and heart-scathing events, consequent upon its early torpor; and I should not be surprised if she should yet come to me across the wastes of life for sympathy and help; for she knew I would fain have given her my time and strength to awaken in her a love of excellence. Such characters have success in the world from very unscrupulousness, till they trample too proudly on the rights of others. The charms they do possess, whether personal or mental, lure them on to greater evils till they are thrown back suddenly into the presence of eternal truth, and then what misery must ensue, what a reckoning must come! Do such children of God see wider and deeper into the eternal truth for having gone astray? I would fain think so; for in this universe of compensations we can only *see that one* for the lost heaven of innocent childhood. Let those who have not such temptations mourn over, but not despise the erring!

I would aid many children to conquer temper by a near penalty, or give courage to confess a fault by taking away the apprehension of all other punishment than the natural one of self-reproach, reflected from the mother-confessor; but sometimes I see children who are afraid of nothing in heaven or earth, the current of whose impertinence I can indeed check for the moment; the bold, defying glance of whose eye I can quell, but the coarse texture of whose mind admits none of the more delicate influences. A large generosity, or a great moral indignation or self-conquest, may be comprehended by such children, but not a fine sympathy, or a tender regret.

I have had pupils with as violent passions, as determined will, as much intellectual insight, and a temperament that made every emotion as keen as the stroke of a Damascus blade, but a sensibility that would respond to the gentlest touch, and a conscience whose stings were like a sharp goad. This keenness of nature made childhood's experience like that of a matured mind that had seen and felt the consequences of evil; and the gravity of age took the place of the buoyancy of childhood. A word in season would bring such a child to repentance and amendment too, for I think nothing of occasional backsliding, where the desire of improvement prevails. Such children are subject to abuse of a peculiar kind, which they seldom escape. This quick sensibility is too often called forth, and a morbid sensitiveness is produced which too often takes refuge in recklessness. I have known such instances where the very words "doing right" became hateful, when uttered by lips that had invaded too often the sacred sensibility. Such vivid intellects are also apt to be exercised too strongly for the entertainment of others, and excited to undue activity by questions of morals which should not be urged thus early, if we wish for a healthful development. The principle of self-government is thus impaired, not strengthened. The trial of strength ought to come later in life; and truthfulness alone will save one who has such painful associations with virtue. I am thinking now of a particular child whose peace of mind I have seen thus disturbed fearfully, and to whom I felt it my duty to secure as much tranquillity as the hours he passed with me could contain, even if advancement in literature must be sacrificed to that end.

I know nothing more painful than to see a child of delicate sensibility, and lively moral sense, growing hardened to the wrong-doing of others, as it grows older, and even learning to expect it. I have seen this in more than one child, and it has made me feel that there is a limit beyond which we should not open the eyes of childhood. Let them live in happy unconsciousness of all evil but that which is in themselves, as long as possible, and let the characters of others be mysterious to them, rather than let them acquire the habit of looking out for blemishes by hearing low motives attributed to others. I would never trace out evil in character before children, except where refraining from doing so might risk the injury of the moral sense. We all know, I fear, what it is to have our idols cast down, and our ideal desecrated and sad; bitter indeed is the wakening from our dream of man-and-woman-worship; but we learn one thing by dwelling upon the perfection of our ideal, and that is, of what we are capable. No one can ever realize that who has not worshipped some fellow-mortal, at some time. I would not forget the passionate loves of my childhood for anything I have yet realized in life.

Upon the whole, if I find truth in a character, I pass lightly over all other deficiencies. And even some forms of falsehood do not discourage me. A child that is managed by strategem will almost inevitably become artful; but a generous, confiding treatment, in which his honor is trusted, will probably bring him back to candor and simplicity. I love to teach children to look upon and understand the virtues of others, to excite their enthusiasm for fearless truth, self-sacrifice, and long-suffering patience and kindness. All the experience of my life is worked up into little stories. When I say "once I knew, &c," I always chain attention. I love to tell of one child I knew when very young, who would never let another child communicate any secret, as children take such pleasure in doing, without saying in answer to the question, "Will you never tell?" "Nobody but my mother." This was her invariable answer, and her sturdiness through all manner of ridicule made a great impression upon me. We were inseparable companions, and I remember nothing that bound me to her so strongly as this uprightness. I adopted the same measure by her advice, and we doubtless escaped much evil in that way. She went by the name of "*Nobody But,*" but she had true moral courage, and I used to resent, in her behalf, this nickname. My loyalty to her generally saved me from even the temptation of being asked. This and other small heroes and heroines are important mythological personages in my school.

I have one scholar who was brought to me from a very large school where no child could receive individual attention, and no subject of interest was either studied or talked about. Certain outward actions brought certain rewards or punishments. The principles of self-government and conscience were never addressed. His mind, of fine natural powers, would have been starved all that time if he had not had intellectual culture at home. When he came into my school-room I could see that every association with such scenes was wearisome and disgusting. Before the study-bell was rung, he would pour into my ear the whole history of his life, his excursions among the mountains, the stories told him by his travelled uncles, his knowledge of animals, birds, flowers, and all in a childlike spirit of confidence in my interest and sympathy, which he caught from the other children. But when the school-hour came, a lassitude pervaded all his faculties, and even a spirit of opposition seemed to take possession of him. It was not the signal for many pleasant things to happen, as with the rest, but for some stupid effort to be made. The memory of many thousand spelling lessons, including countless words to which no idea was attached in his mind, and of dull readings of the same uninteresting sentences from the beginning to the end of the year, and the adding, subtracting, and dividing of inexpressive numbers, came thronging thick upon him. I learned the facts from outside testimony, first suspecting them from their effects. It needed only to look at him to see them written in his expressive face.

As soon as I saw clearly how it was, I determined that my school-room should for a time be as much like the wild woods as I could make it, consistently with due decorum; that he should enjoy the sweets of liberty in certain ways, while at the same time I would endeavor gently to substitute for his previous associations with study, something more living. I soon saw that he evidently thought he was to do pretty much as he pleased. I did not always check him when he walked to the window without any apparent object but to enjoy the prospect in the street, though I sometimes expressed surprise that he should do it when I had given him a lesson to learn. He saw no black marks expressive of the youthful sins of looking up from his book, or treading on the toes of his neighbors, though after a while I gave him a little table by himself, because he had not self-control enough to refrain from such interference with others. I once remarked to him that he was like those people whom society put into the State-prison, because he violated social duties. Only those could enjoy freedom who did not interfere with others' rights and comforts. The taste for liberty soon spread into other things. He did not like to study anything that required an effort, and showed a great feeling of discouragement whenever anything new was required of him. He always said "can't," and often added in a half whisper, "wont." I did not yield to this, but insisted upon having my requisitions answered, partly because obedience must be the cardinal virtue in school, and partly because I knew such despondency would never be conquered unless by a sense of power to conquer difficulties. Much time and labor it cost me and him to establish my authority in this respect, and to induce him to begin to study a hard lesson. After I had gained these points, however, I gradually set aside those things to which he had the most aversion, and which had no interest but one borrowed from a sense of duty, and thought it best to let him choose more for himself. I could have done this earlier if the aversion to certain mental efforts had not been accompanied with wilful resistance to my wishes, and a want of consideration for my duties. Many of the vile tricks of school-boys, both in school and in play-hours, annoyed me and his companions.

At last the reaction began to take place. He became interested in Latin fables and natural history, and when I began to administer less interesting things in small doses, he would bring his book to me saying, "I can't tell how to get this lesson," instead of "I shall never get this, and I am not going to try." When I found he could adopt a suggestion from me as to the best way to conquer a difficulty, I could send him into another room to pronounce French phrases aloud, without the interruption of other recitations. I had no possible penalties for the recurrence of fits of idleness, and when he interrupted others, I only expressed my surprise and regret that he should be so childish and selfish, and occasionally sent him home because he was utterly disagreeable. These faults seemed to be the result of a morbid activity where healthful manifestations had been arbitrarily checked, and not an evil disposition; for he really loved little children, and was communicating and confiding to me before and after school, quite courteous and polite to me as Miss P——, but wholly in opposition to the school-dame. I always took pains to appeal to him for his traveller's stories when they came in appropriately to the geography lesson, or could illustrate in any way what was read. School began gradually to afford him the same sort of pleasure he received from reading with his mother, which was always agreeable, and had stored his mind with pleasant knowledge. In morals as well as in lessons I did the same thing. I called upon him to help me take care of the little children when we walked, because I saw he could do this with ease and pleasure. As soon as any other relation took the place of the school relation, all things went on agreeably. He knew that I respected his word, and that his story had due weight in the scale when I asked for various testimony in regard to any subject of difference.

My object was, as you will perceive, to leave him to feel the natural consequences of doing wrong, instead of fearing any arbitrary punishment; being confident that the natural sequence of things (that is, God's arrangements) would enlighten the mind as no mere penalty or mere precept could do. I often feel that I can see the prominent points in a case like this, where a mother may not, owing to her position. Neither do mothers know the faults of the school-room. I give information of these, as they tell me the faults of the nursery. Children that cry much in nurseries, seldom cry at all in a school-room, where a pleasing variety occupies the time, and a seed-grain of self-control is planted; and temptations arise in the school-room, where peculiar efforts and sacrifices are called for, that do not assail the child at home. The mother of this boy could hardly be made to believe that in school-hours neither his intellect nor his conscience acted, because she knew they did at other times. It was as if a spell bound him there. In his previous school-life there had been little but spelling-lessons, and what is called discipline, which consists, as far as I can understand, (and I have inquired very particularly of those who advocate the system,) of teaching as many uninteresting words as can be crowded into the memory, especial care being taken to keep out of the way all ideas. It was in such a conversation that the view was advanced to which I have before alluded, that the less interest, the more discipline of study. The advocate of such a plan thought everything that was studied in youth was forgotten, be it what it might, therefore training (alias misery and waste of time) was alone useful or desirable. He instanced his own experience as a proof of this, and where it was gently insinuated that perhaps if those forgotten geography lessons, Latin lessons, etc., had had any interest of their own, such as associations with interesting people, or the amusement of a story, they might have kept their place in his mind, he rejected the idea entirely, showing, as the Puritans did when they persecuted the Quakers for doing the very thing they had done, the evils of a bad education. I even ventured a little story, (that being a lively kind of argument I like to use,) of a little girl in my school, who, when I was endeavoring to make her hear the thunder-music and see the rainbow-tinted spray of Niagara Falls, exclaimed, "Why, I never knew before that Niagara Falls was made of water!" — but I found he could not be taught "out of the mouth of babes and sucklings."

I could have told him, if I had not been discouraged, of a dear little boy of my acquaintance, seven years old, whom his mother wished to send to my school, but his more ambitious father chose to put him into the Latin Grammar-School, (the very one of which this gentleman was usher when I talked with him.) His mother begged me to let him come to me privately to learn with me the terrible Latin Grammar-lesson of three pages, which was to be his first lesson in the school, and the language. So little Georgie and I had a secret session every day for a long time, in which we got the lesson together — I would hear him say it, and he would hear me, and I endeavored to extract some hidden meaning from it for him, but although I saved him from many a feruling, his hatred of school became so intense, from the impossibility he found of ever succeeding without penalty and suffering, that he actually broke down in spirits and health, and was at last taken away and sent to a military school to save his life. His mother and I knew why he failed, for he was of delicate organization, easily frightened, and his sensibility, which was keen and might have opened to him the beauties of the universe, was poisoned and embittered by unjust severity and the fearful drill of that model school. Some of my boys who have gone there after having learned to use their faculties, have succeeded well, and found no difficulties; but poor little George was taken from what I call a spelling-school, and put into that tread-mill, as it proved to him. I attribute a subsequent unhappy career to this mistake in his education, but I hope something will yet evoke his originally lovely nature.*

When one hears such views as these, and many others of similar import that I could recount, one almost despairs of ever seeing a whole man. The fact that there is a grain of truth in such heaps of falsehood, only increases the difficulty, because that grain of truth prevents the recognition of that mass of error. My observation and experience are that, not till things are intelligently learned do they begin to fertilize the mind, or are they even sure to stay in it, and scarcely a fine intellect will give you any other record of itself than that the date of its improvement began at that era when either

* Since writing the above he has died untimely.

self-education or the wise teacher showed it the thread of relation that runs through all things. Not till at least one human fact has exemplified some spiritual law, does the intellect work intelligently, or begin to arrange its stores. Do we not know some minds that are mere encyclopedias, which imagination has never penetrated with its Ithuriel spear? If such have moral sense in any fair proportion, they are liable to become hopelessly miserable in this world of shadows because they can see nothing but the shadows.

I once knew a mother who was a beautiful type to me of the spirit that should actuate the guardians of the young. She looked upon a soul with such awe that it was not easy for her to impose her authority upon her children, for might there not be something in their natures superior to her own? The possibility of this made her cautious in her requisitions, lest she should nip some beautiful bud of promise in them. I knew her when they were all young, and I saw that it was not want of decision, but the fear of doing harm that often arrested her action. The children were not always serene and happy, and sometimes not obedient, for they had strong wills, and what is called a great deal of character. How could there but be strong individuality in such a family? There was no fixed pattern by which they were all to be measured. But they reverenced her as she did them, for she lived and acted simply and genuinely, and encompassed them round about with her tenderness, practising daily those virtues of devotion and self-denial which are demanded of the mother of a large family, and never turning a deaf ear to the wants of those less favored with earthly happiness than herself. She treated her children with the respect one human being owes to another, irrespective of age. Yet she did not commit the error we sometimes see of reasoning out every point of duty with children, thus teaching them to quibble and catch at words. She could check that while she showed respect for their reasons. She had that true humility which makes its possessors question every step of the way in the path of duty, while they have a trusting faith that there is something within them to answer to its calls.

She died suddenly, and then her influence, which many might have doubted, appeared in a wonderful and beautiful manner. Circumstances were such that no one was able to take the proper care of the family for a month or two in the absence of the father. The eldest children, two boys, one fourteen, the other eleven, immediately took the place of their mother as a matter of course, assumed the personal care which they had seen their mother take every day, of six little brothers and sisters, arranging everything as their mother had done, even in such minutiæ as placing the clothes in the proper drawers, and washing and dressing the younger children, which the mother had never left to servants, although the home was well supplied with them. In a quiet and unostentatious manner a large establishment had been managed by a superior mind so skilfully, that these boys found no difficulty in keeping everything in train till their father's return. They had been inspired by their mother with a sense of order, propriety, and responsibility, for it was a peculiarity in her that she rather acted than inculcated principles, and through their great and tender affection, which had been her happiness in life, her characteristics flowed naturally and without a break into their lives. Such a mother should every teacher be, especially of young children.

You need not tell me that mothers and teachers must be wise as well as tender, courageous as well as reverential. I know it well. I can tell you of a young mother who risked an essential injury to her child (humanly speaking, for we cannot injure the *essence* of another) by allowing him to quibble upon subjects of right and wrong, and accepting his excuses when he could found them upon any inadvertence of hers. His mental motions were more rapid than hers, and a morbid tenderness of conscience made her hesitate to lay injunctions upon him, lest she might err in judgment. A natural tendency to subtlety and stratagem was thus fostered in him, and as he had not much imagination, there was danger that he would become actually deceitful. He led an innocent life compared with many boys of his age, for he was kept very much out of harm's way, but I soon perceived the pleasure he experienced from a successful trick of fun, and that his great command over his nerves tempted him to play many such, which he could do with a grave face. I never saw one that was not in itself innocent fun, and if they had been practised as some children practise them, who will betray their agency the next moment from mere artlessness, I should only have battled the point with him as I do with others who play in school in study hours, (or rather half hours.) But I saw that this was likely to become a deeper evil, connected as it was with his habit of excusing himself, finding flaws in my directions, and quibbling upon words. It was too serious a matter for penalties of my device, designed as reminders, nor was I willing to enter the lists with him and vanquish him by my superior sagacity, for this would be only sharpening his tools.

I took a good opportunity one day to call what he did *mean*, and to tell him that I thought he was growing cunning, which I was very sorry for, as that led to deception of all sorts. It was very funny to pull another boy's hair, and then look grave as if he knew nothing about it, which I had often seen him do, but I could not laugh at fun, when it was at the expense of truthfulness, though I enjoyed a good joke as well as any one. It was wrong, too, for him to play when I was looking the other way, because it was cheating me and setting a bad example to the other scholars. I liked to be able to trust people's honor, and when I gave a direction, and then went to the other side of the room to attend to others, in the confidence that my wishes would be conscientiously regarded, I was disappointed and grieved to find that I was cheated. I did not like to be obliged to watch people. I could not respect any one I must watch, and I would not watch him. If he would do wrong and teach others to do so, he must sit entirely by himself. As to himself, no one else could cure him of his faults. If he was willing to grow deceitful, no one could help it; but if he had no honor, every one must defend himself against him, and he could command no respect from any one, nor have any of his own, which I thought more precious than that of others. What was a person good for who could not have self-respect? It was a pleasant thing to make other people laugh, but if he could allow another to bear the blame of it, and not speak up to say he was the offender, I could not trust him even when he did speak. I added, that I had long observed these tricks of his, and had been sure they would at last lead to meanness, and here was an instance of it just as I had expected. I also reminded him of an occasion when I saw him take an unfair advantage in play for the mere pleasure of winning a little game, thus giving up his honor for the enjoyment of a moment. I hoped he would remember these instances and the danger to which he was exposing himself. I would not dare to punish such faults, for I might be suspicious of him when he did not deserve it, as I could not always read his mind or be sure of his sincerity. The punishment must be the one God had appointed for such faults — and that was, a loss of integrity itself, the most dreadful of all punishments.

The child loved me and thought a great deal of my opinion. He did not wish the tears in his eyes to fall, and he swallowed them till his face flushed. I had spoken before all the school, as it was a public offence not to be passed over; for nothing is more attractive to children than the wittiness of practical jokes, as I knew one child to confess when asked which boys he liked best in a certain story, "Oh the bad boys," said he, "I like the wittiness of them."

I afterwards took every opportunity to put this little fellow upon his honor, and often said, so that he might hear it, that if any one wished to be fair and honorable, they had better not indulge in what seemed very innocent fun when concealment was necessary, for fear of learning to deceive. I often appealed to him for testimony, because I knew he had accuracy of observation, and dwelt particularly on such occasions upon my wish that he should tell me all his own part in a transaction, very carefully, both good and bad, for the sake of helping me to do justice, and urged him not to be cowardly, or keep back anything for fear of being blamed. Blame, I once told him, was one of our best friends. The fear of it sometimes kept us from doing wrong even when we had no better reason, and when we had done wrong, it showed us to ourselves, just as we were, and waked conscience up to its duty. Only cowards were afraid to tell the truth against themselves. Yet I checked him whenever he *told tales* of others; which is a thing I always carefully discriminate from telling the truth when asked. I checked him also because one of his bad habits was to excuse himself, and the temptation that assailed him was to throw the blame on others.

In every way I could think of, I thus tried to show him how his particular tendencies would lead him into falsehood, which I *assumed* to be the greatest of faults.

After three years' continuance in my school, I assure you there was not a child in it that I would more readily trust, and though he always annoyed me with his playfulness, it ceased to be tricky. I had frequent occasions to notice his candor and to refer to his improvement. I never spoke to him again before the school upon the subject of his mean fault, but I kept it fresh in his own mind, and long after, when I reproved another child for symptoms of the same fault, I remarked that one of my scholars had once given me the same cause to fear for his integrity, but he had watched himself, and I was glad to say he had resisted temptation and grown honorable and trustworthy. I saw that he knew who I meant, but the others had forgotten who it could be. I did not gratify their curiosity, of course.

I do not know that this boy is above temptation, but I

have had many proofs of his power to resist it; occasions that brought him no glory, some of which I have recognized by such a remark as "how respectable honesty is," or "how I like to see moral courage that fears nothing but doing wrong." Sometimes I took no visible notice, for we need not always praise well-doing. It is often both unnecessary and unwise, for where goodness is not wholly spontaneous, it may be vitiated by love of approbation. It is only *perfect* goodness, or such measure of that as mortals may attain, that can always bear praise and grow only more fervent for it.

Sometimes I leave one scholar to keep school while I go into another room to hear a lesson, and then I require an account of their stewardship. I am always careful to select one whom all will concur in respecting and of whom they will feel no jealousy when they are censured. I once left this boy in charge, but after a short time he came and requested to be released, because he felt as if it was like tale-bearing to tell of his companions, and he did not feel sure that they would be willing. I saw by this that he meant to be faithful; indeed, it was not till after I had full confidence in him that I ventured on so important a step. I presume he did not feel as if I could say, as I had said of some others, "You know —— would not find fault with you if he could help it, or if his conscience did not require it of him." There is no point that must be managed with such delicacy as this of discriminating between truth and falsehood. Children live so long in their ideal worlds, and are so much talked to in symbols, that when they begin to deal more with realities they must often be reminded to be accurate. I would lead them gently out of the creations of their imaginations when this time comes, constantly reminding them that they must tell things just as they are; and when they embellish their statements, I go over them quietly, re-stating for them, and leaving out all the marvellous additions. Little children will often quote their absent mothers' authority, when it is impossible that the circumstances can have been anticipated. I always reply to this very decidedly, "Oh! no; mother did not say so. She does not know anything about it; you must not tell me so; that is saying what is not true, which is very wrong." If they persist, I say, "Very well; I will write a little note to mother when you go home, and tell her I am afraid her little child has said what is not true, shall I?" This will generally bring out a confession. I do not punish on such occasions, for there is no surer way of producing falsehood than by inspiring fear, but I try to produce a little agony in the conscience and make a child very unhappy for the moment. This suffering can be referred to afterwards, in private, and the danger pointed out of growing wicked, which I find the greatest instrument of awakening the inward monitor.

Some people object to allegories and fairy stories for children, but I am never afraid of them if they are true to nature, truly imaginative, or if the impossible is occasionally caught a glimpse of. A fairy that comes out of a flower, is an imaginary being that will never disturb the dreams or deceive the intellect of a child. I always call such stories poetry, and sometimes ask what they teach. If a teaching use cannot be made of them, they are not written conscientiously and are not good food for the young. A child of well cultivated imagination will be likely to be more rather than less truthful than others. But I do not like ogres. I once had a scholar, a child of eleven years, that had never known the care of parents. She was a southern child, whose parents died in her infancy, and she was sent from one boarding-school to another, where she was made the tool of unscrupulous girls to obtain their ends against authority. She told untruths *always*, even upon the most trivial matters, as if she feared being circumvented, or giving any handle to others by whom she might be blamed. She was so subtle, that it was almost impossible to obtain a fact from her, although she lived in the family. Her relations had wholly neglected all personal care of her, and I found she knew nothing whatever about them. I learned that her parents were two very lovely young people, both of whom died early of consumption, and she had an uncle who was a bachelor and a very wealthy planter. He had been very fond of his sister, and meant to take home this child and make her his heiress as soon as she was old enough. She had the precocity of constitution and temperament common to the southerners, but had no interest in life at all except for present gratification. It was difficult to interest her in anything, and I determined to try the experiment of describing her parents and her uncle, and telling her of her future prospects. I saw when I was talking to her that she was much moved, but she did not wish me to know it. During the several months she had been under my care, I had never seen her off her guard, and she did not mean to be now. She said, "yes, I know," several times, but in her emotion she had forgotten that she had told me several times when I had asked her, that she had no relations. As I went on speaking of the lovely character of her mother, who died at her birth, I saw the color flash and her lips quiver, but she would express no interest in the matter in words, and I took no notice of her natural emotions. But when I went on to speak of the uncle and his beautiful home, his love for his sister, and for her, whom he had never seen since her babyhood, and of his wish that she should preside over his home when old enough, she fairly burst into tears; and when I drew her into my arms she put her head on my bosom and gave way to violent sobbing. But still she was cautious in speaking, and I did not convict her of having concealed the truth. She was naturally very timid, and I had divined the cause of her phase of falsehood. She had been treated very cruelly, and was afraid of human beings. After a while she proposed to write to her uncle and tell him what she was studying; but although I doubt not life had a new interest to her, I could not tell what was the characteristic of her interest, owing to her great reserve. It might have been sordid, for she was very selfish; but she was soon removed, and I had no opportunity of seeing her for many years. I then found her still in the family of her guardian, to one of whose sons she was engaged, but I was told there was no love, only speculation, at the foundation of the young man's views, and the seeds of consumption, inherited from her mother, had begun to ripen in her. She was brilliantly beautiful, and showed a great deal of feeling on seeing me, but died very soon after. The only evidence I ever had of the existence of the moral sentiment in her wronged soul, was her fondness for another child in my family, who was the soul of truth and love, and who had divine patience with this her little tormentor, whom she watched over and remonstrated with like a little mother. This companion, of just her own age, had had a very remarkable moral training, consecrated forever by the sufferings for conscience' sake of a very dear and gifted mother, whose persecutions were known to her child, and no one could know her, not even the most hardened or obtuse, without being affected by her. She was a little Christ among other children, and so regarded by them, and I always hoped that the poor little waif had through her a glimpse of the Heaven into which she seemed to have no passport. At the time, I rejoiced for my little angel, when her heart was relieved of such a charge, for certain natural graces as well as the condition of moral benightment of the little stranger had taken very deep hold of her; but I think a reform might have been effected with such an aid. The martyr's child lived long enough to fulfil her promise, and grew happy enough to blossom out into some buds of lovely promise, intellectual as well as moral, and then she went too, but could be no more an angel the other side of the veil than she was on this. How slight the barrier sometimes seems to be, yet how impervious! Was it the *divine love* in you which made you do that? was her mother's form of reproof, always *remembered.*

Is there any danger of inspiring a child with too great self-reliance, by directing it to the immutable law of God in its own breast as a guide of conduct? It has been wisely said that we know of the moral nature of God only what the moral sentiment teaches us, and that the visible world and revelation only confirm what this sentiment gives primarily. We know that the sentiment of reverence may be directed to objects unworthy the homage of the soul. In the fluctuations of human opinion there may be a higher or lower view of God's nature. He may be looked upon as all justice without mercy, or as mercy without justice, or as a union of both, according to the enlightenment of the intellect, but we can cultivate in every child a reverence for God's voice in conscience, an allegiance to God as goodness itself, or as a Father, ready to forgive us when we repent, and to help our efforts. The human being may by turns worship God as a Father, as a power, or as law; and salvation, or the redemption of the soul from evil, does not depend upon the form of belief, but upon the allegiance to that something higher which is a law to it. I do not say that it is not important what the form is, for we know that there is all the difference in the world between the savage's worship of his fetish, and the Christian's of his God, but the savage may be more loyal to the small glimmer of truth represented by his fetish, than many a so-called Christian is to his more advanced conception of Deity. Therefore it is loyalty of soul which is to be cultivated, and that is done through conscience.

I know no higher motive to be given to a child or to a man, than that the more he obeys the voice of conscience, the more tender it becomes; and the more he cultivates his intellect the greater will be its expansion; and no fear that either can entertain is so salutary as the fear of losing the delicacy of the conscience, or the power of increasing insight.

Offer no secondary motives, but as high a view as we can give of the primal one, not judging for our fellow-man, or even child, what it is ready to receive, for either may be capable of receiving more than we can give.

This does not interfere with bringing the consequences of wrong-doing into immediate view, which is in fact all that we do when we punish judiciously. If a child is selfish he is thrust aside by those who have the power to do it. This is a direct natural consequence, quite as much so as that the selfishness grows by indulgence, but weak children in a school or in a family must not venture to thrust aside an offender. I must therefore come to their assistance.

I have one child in my school who has so little power of self-control, that I am obliged to be very peremptory with him every day. It would not be sufficient for me to say, "You trouble others so that they do not like to have you sit near them," and wait for that truth to influence him. I must put him in a seat by himself, and show him that he is not to approach others now, and that he must make an immediate effort to gain a better social position. If anything comes into his head, he seems utterly incapable of refraining from the utterance of it, even in the midst of a recitation, or be it ever so irrelevant to the matter in hand. He wishes to tell anecdotes of which he is reminded by something read or recited. If I tell him he must not take up the time, he is so earnest to go on, that often I cannot stop him without walking him out of the room. Then I tell him that since he has no power of self-control, he must stay there till I call him; or I allow him to return on condition that he does not open his mouth even to read or to recite. I impose this privation to teach him self-control, the want of which will make him annoying to every one. He pours forth many sensible remarks and more good feelings, but the law of adaptation seems wanting. He has sensibility and conscience, and a general desire to do right. If not approved, he is afflicted; if he does not succeed in his undertakings, he cries with grief, cries aloud often, though a huge boy of nine years old, — a little giant in form and strength. He generally seems to tell the truth, though he is weak, and yields easily to the temptation of gaining his ends. But if he cannot remember easily, he lashes himself into hysterics. He has quick perceptive powers, but little power of reasoning. My aim is to show him the connection between his faults and his sufferings; to let the latter be felt to be the whip that scourges his faults — not himself; for there is no fair proportion between the constant punishment he brings upon himself and his wilful wrong-doing. I am afraid he will always be a trial to his friends. He is one of my least hopeful cases, because not well gifted. I am afraid there is a germ somewhere that the sun has not yet shone upon — that some tile that is now weighing down his brain must be lifted before mortal man can help him. You remember the story of Descartes, who was an idiot till his skull was cracked, when suddenly the brain expanded, and the fissure never closing, he became a great man. Perhaps my obtuse boy will get some friendly blow, mental or physical, that will let in the light. His mother turned him out into the street to amuse himself, because she could not manage him. If she had not, perhaps I should already have turned him back upon her hands, for he really is the greatest trouble I have. My hope for him is that maturity and experience will teach him what others cannot. This is often the case.

Another little fellow appears to have no natural perception of the rights of others. He does not understand the sentiment of obedience, as many lively children do. If I keep my eye fixed upon him, he does not do the things I positively forbid him to do, but he is the very prince of mischief, and I am obliged to watch him narrowly lest he turn inkstands upside down, and go to such like extremes. In some cases I merely follow my instincts, and this is such an one. I feel as if I were to put principle into this child because I have it myself, much as the magnetist imposes his will upon his patient by exercising it forcibly. I find myself looking at him much more than I talk to him, not always reprovingly, never stealthily, but steadily and gravely. I do not like to govern, but I am not afraid of children, as some people are. My nerves can bear their crying, if they do not cry with pain, and they soon learn that they gain nothing from me by it. They do not put me out of temper, or exhaust my patience, or my perseverance; but the determined will, the ever-springing gayety, the wild spirits that tire most people, are a constant source of pleasure and exhilaration to me. It seems to me so unnatural that childhood should be naughty, that if they are obstinate I am very apt to think it the fault of some still more obstinate grown person, who has turned a stout heart into a wilful one by unwise opposition; and I love to set myself to disarming the stubborn will, leaving it only resolute. If they are false, I feel as if their faith had been broken, or their fears excited, and I love to show them the beauty of truth, or inspire them with moral courage. If they are passionate, I love to calm them down, and give them the pleasure of tranquillity, and the joys of self-conquest, — not "breaking their spirits," but sympathizing with their ardor while I check its excesses; for enthusiasm is a boon of which I would not deprive humanity. If they are phlegmatic, commonly called stupid, I love to find some subject or object of interest that will startle them into animation; if timid and easily discouraged, I can give them the pleasures of success by offering only practicable tasks; if self-conceited, I can point out to them the kingdoms of knowledge yet to be conquered. I often quote the words of Linnæus, who once said it would take him all his life to learn thoroughly what was under his own hand, and what was this compared with the universe!

I believe I enjoy the youngest of my tribe most, before they know evil or are accustomed to hear of it with composure; when the wanton killing of a bird, or even of a spider, excites their weeping indignation; when the creations of their own fancies are as real to them as the things before their bodily eyes; and they do not question if the bird in the story speaks, or the stars sing. One may then imagine that they may be among the few who love to the end with unbroken faith, who never lose their primitive innocence, but grow as the tree grows, whose leaves, when the early frost nips them, turn to scales to protect their sister growths, adding to the final perfection of the whole, not arresting its beautiful and symmetrical progress, neither withering in the bud, nor throwing out gnarled branches to the light and heat that would fain warm and smile upon them. I would not pin these little inheritors of the earth to one seat, or always check the wild burst of delight, or the ringing laugh. I even like to have the older children hear it occasionally, and recognize it with a smile as I do, for they have already begun to *remember* happiness, alas! as if it had already begun its flight. They have laughed when it was not sympathized with, been reproved for loving fun, and deprived of innocent sports because they were not convenient to others. I like to keep up their sympathies with the spontaneous activity and pure imaginations of these babes. It is out of order for a little child that catches my eye to run across the room to say, "Oh, may I come and see 'oo 'ittle while?" but I cannot but nod assent, and he will come and scramble into my lap, where he is no sooner fairly settled and hugged than he will scramble down again and go back to his slate or his window. If he nestles up into his sister's chair, while she is studying, I put my finger on my lips, but let her put her arm round him and keep him till he is tired. This little sunbeam begins to wish to draw on the slate, and the little sister of seven years takes the greatest interest in what he does, as if expecting some angelic exploit of the pencil.

But though I wish to have self-government in my scholars instead of my own, dear Anna, do not for a moment mistake me. I consider obedience an essential ingredient of order, and order I regard as "heaven's first law." Indeed I have sent away one scholar of whom I have spoken a little way back, because I could not command his obedience; and my authority must not be questioned, although I do not obtrude it. No human being can be good or happy who cannot obey; and those parents do the best thing for their children, who successfully cultivate the sentiment. For, if it is the *sentiment*, it will acknowledge all lawful authority. When it is merely a practice gained through fear, there is generally no sentiment in it. The child who will not eat the bit of cake offered in its mother's absence, because she has refused to let him have it before, — and I have known many such, — is truly the obedient child. Children not only respect most but love best those whom they cheerfully obey. A child that obeys a judicious and affectionate mother, or teacher, will often, in the midst of its opposition and wilfulness, acknowledge that the power which rules him is a beneficent power. If I did not think that a pretty good child would feel that I was in the right very soon after a conflict of wills, I should suspect myself of having given some evidence of love of power or want of good temper. I would not restrain an expression of honest indignation, or strong disapprobation, if the offence deserved it; but any impatience of temper, or any personal feeling, except that of sorrow, is a crime in this relation. It may not be in a mother's or teacher's power to be always wise, judicious, or intellectually ready for an occasion; but the virtue of patience is lawfully demanded of them at the tribunal of conscience always. Corporal punishment I have nothing to do with, for though I know it is necessary in some extreme cases, I prefer that parents should exercise that function. No person that has a less vital interest in a child than a parent, should inflict it; and though as a principle of government I consider it brutalizing, there are instances in which I have felt it to be a *holy* act, and in which I have known the child to respect it, and to feel hurt for its parent rather than for itself. But my own influence, to be secure and useful, must be wholly moral and intellectual. I often tell children that I must inform their parents when I find them impervious to any influence of mine; and when, as has sometimes been the case, they have begged me not to do it, because they should be whipped, I have said that "perhaps that was the very best possible thing that could be done, and if a parent thought it necessary to whip his child, it must be because he truly loved him, and thought it right to do what must be to himself a painful thing: such a reason must not deter me from doing my duty. I should not act according to my conscience if I concealed anything from parents, for they are the guardians God has appointed over children, and I should do wrong to prevent them from knowing everything that I knew, that would help them make their children good."

I cannot provide for those exceptional cases illustrated to me by a little new scholar I once had, who was very refractory. I said to him, "don't you wish to be good, Lewis?" "No," he cried out in a distressed voice. He was only six years old, but this seemed to be a new case, so I put my arm affectionately round him and said, "What does it mean to be good, Lewis?" He raised his tearful eyes to me and gasped out "ter be whipped!" I never saw a look of greater infantile woe; but I soon taught him that that was not what I meant by "being good."

I know one mother who has a family of excitable children, which she treats wholly on hygienic principles. If they are out of temper, she administers nauseous doses of medicine, and such has been her power over their consciences that she can make them grateful to God for such blessings as ipecacuanha and epsom salts, even when she is holding the spoon to their mouths. This is a fact within my knowledge; and it was the first thing I knew that set my thoughts upon the track, which has led me to a firm conviction that half the ills of temper and perversity may be traced to physical causes; for her instinct proved to be a correct one. Her children were honorable and affectionate, but irritable, and this was owing to an unhappy inheritance of physical structure, incompatible with serenity till counteracted by judicious treatment. One of those wise physicians, who sometimes adorn the profession, was her aid and counsellor. "Her children rise up and call her blessed," and bless her too.

LETTER VI.

Dear Anna, — I have just heard that you think of changing your original plan, and becoming a governess. At the risk of being impertinent, I must give you the warning of experience against this course. I know the voice of experience is not an unerring one, because circumstances differ almost infinitely, but I think the relation of governess an unnatural one, and also that the disadvantages of home education, given exclusively, far overbalance its advantages. Mark me, I say given exclusively, for I think the early education should always be domestic. I would have every mother set apart from all the other duties of life to attend to her children, and be qualified to give them the rudiments of not only moral but intellectual training. I know only one mother who has done this absolutely and with all the requisite surroundings, though I know many who would be glad to do it. Perhaps I should say I know only one father who has made it possible. Doubtless there are some fathers who would be glad to have it done, with whom the mothers are not ready to coöperate. I could branch off here, and tell all I think about parents not having the right views of their parental duties, but that would take me still farther back, to the subject of being married on the right principles, which I have been led to reflect much upon, as I have circulated through the families of my friends, particularly of those who have from time to time put their children into my charge. I speak it with diffidence, but I see many families in which the children are regarded in the light of annoyances rather than of blessings; consequently they are penned up in nurseries, put to bed by servants, fed by them, washed and dressed by them, excused by them, falsely entertained by them, in fact educated by them, until they are old enough to be quiet inmates of the parlor, when they are allowed to be present to listen to conversations about the last new fashion, or comments upon the party of last night and that of the night to come. I have known the mothers of children under my care, to promise a sick child she would not go out in the evening, in order to quiet her querulous complaints of her nurse or attendant, and then to break the promise as soon as the child fell asleep, confiding in its mother's sincerity. This is an extreme case, but it is not so rare for mothers to send their children to bed under the care of servants, instead of leaving the pleasant fireside to make the most of that gracious hour when the heart of the child is most likely to unfold to the tender parent, and to utter its repentant confession or fervent little prayer.

But this is wandering a little from the point. I begin to think I indulge in too many digressions; but my vocation leads me into such observations and reflections.

I know there is much to be said on both sides of this question. I should give you the sum of my opinion, if I should say that after the age has arrived at which children are ordinarily sent to school, an alternation of the home and the school education is the best mode. Here experience raises her voice again; for the best educations I have known, all other things being equal, have been in two families where this has been done. In one of these, the watchful eye of the mother saw the very moment in which the home influence was becoming too exclusive and oppressive, and also when the school influence became scattering to the mind from too much companionship, or when ambition took the place of love of knowledge and excellence. The school intercourse was occasionally broken in upon by months of home life, when the mother devoted herself as companion in study and recreation, and kept alive her daughters' sympathy with her in her domestic duties. I have often seen the mere school-life kill out this sympathy with mothers and younger members of the family, and foreign influences quite counteract the parental ones.

My own favorite mode of education would be to send children to school after they have been well trained in imagination and self control at home, at the age when the social feeling seeks variety, and can receive least injury from indiscriminate contact; and when arrived at the age when too much companionship becomes dangerous, to call the girls back to the home influences, and let them there pursue, with judicious assistance, or even a chosen companion, the studies best adapted to the peculiarities of character, the mother ever keeping herself the chosen confidant, and making herself a willing sacrifice, instead of allowing the social tendencies of her daughters to expend themselves on frivolous or unworthy companions. Mothers are too apt to indulge their own ease, and allow their children to frequent, alone, scenes of amusement over which parents should always preside. I have known marriage relations to be formed and cemented by daughters so neglected, before parents knew even the fact of acquaintanceship.

I know how difficult is such practice as I would recommend, in our present state of society; but one can hardly help following out one's imaginings of perfect circumstances, and fancying all the good that might accrue in such millenniums. It was very sensibly remarked to me a little while since, by one to whom I was speaking of my ideal of education for girls, that we can rarely begin and go on with them according to any one system; for they are brought to us in all stages of development, most frequently, alas, without any. You will please always to understand me as if everything went on right from the beginning.

To return to your present plans. I think I must have learnt this rambling habit which so often leads my pen off the track, when roving the woods and fields in my extreme youth, now resting by the side of the arrowy river of my favorite valley, where the "sweet waters meet," or floating with you down the placid Charles at the winds' and the tides' sweet will.

I anticipate what you will tell me of the advantages under which you enter upon the career of a governess. I expect a glowing description of your new life, because I know how you love and admire those friends; but that will make no difference in my views. I too have a friend with whom I agree upon the subject of education; a mother whose experience and wisdom have aided me much, and whose spirit has presided over my school-room as a sort of tutelary genius, into whose family I should be willing to go and give all the aid I could furnish for the furtherance of her plans, (her own book-knowledge not being equal to mine,) if she constituted the whole influence in her own family. There would be a perfect coöperation between us two, the intercourse of years having prepared the way for it. But her husband is not as wise as she is, and I would not therefore venture. Yours may be a peculiar case of sympathy with both parents, but let us look upon it in a general way.

We will suppose a good family, and that the parents are conscientious, and have a general confidence in the judgment and acquirements of the governess. But if the mother is a person of decided views, and fixed in her own opinions, and the father also, you might immediately find insuperable difficulties. You would not like to exert any influence opposed to the parental, however injudicious you might deem that to be. You would not like to take sides with either parent. They might, by amicable discussion, modify each other's views, so as to do just right by their children; while the influence of another, thrown into either scale, would produce dissatisfaction. In your school-room, on the contrary, you can be perfectly independent of either, and without standing in the attitude of opposition, or running the risk of encroaching upon the rights of a parent, you can know just as much and just as little as you please of the difference of views; and having your scholar in a new scene, and subjected to different influences, you may be able fully to carry out your own views, without exciting the jealousy of parents. This is the only way to avoid such collisions as I dread, and which seem to me almost inevitable in such a union as that of parent and teacher in the same family. As an independent teacher, your opinions may be expressed with the utmost freedom; for I would have no tampering with truth. But few mothers are humble or wise enough to be willing to be criticised at home when it comes to the point. Then in my opinion such an inmate spoils a family, which should be a sacred circle where none intrude. I myself have had the whole care of children in a family, moral and intellectual, but no one but the parents ought to have had it. It set up an authority that was more respected than that of the parent. I have also, in another instance, had the sympathy and confidence of one parent, and the jealous watchfulness of the other, who would not listen to the suggestions of a third person. I have also seen children who knew more of truth than their parents, and who knew that I knew it; and I would never again put myself in that position. I have seen the wounded vanity of otherwise good mothers baffle the best intentions and wisest action on the part of a governess; and even sadder cases, where conscience itself must have been sacrificed to keep the peace. No individual should ever step between parents and children, and point out the errors of the former. Principles alone should do this; nothing less sacred should intervene. In my school-room, I can dwell upon principles forever, and apply them to the cases in hand as closely and as skilfully as I please, and keep clear of personalities, if I find them baneful. If one is in the family, this seems to me scarcely possible. Often when I speak of a wrong action, be it the wanton killing of a bird, or the indulgence of an evil passion, children say to me, "My father does that sometimes," and even add, "I wish he would not." This moral judgment is inevitable; it must come sooner or later, and the sooner the child defines the line by his own observations and reflections the better, but it must often pass without comment. I should be sorry to be obliged to be silent upon any point of right and wrong, because there are sinners at my elbow. In a school-room, which is a separate world within the great world, — connected with it, yet severed from it, — principles may reign triumphant. In a family, persons prevail more or less, and this is one of my chief reasons for objecting to an exclusively private education. Special modes of thought and standards of action are imposed by example and habit; and where there is no variety of views presented for comparison, minds cannot easily expand, still less choose the best of several good ways. I have seen the victims of private education perpetuate family faults, and in later life left standing alone in the world, knowing little of its interests, and having no sympathy from without. I have seen morbid sensibility thus nourished into insanity itself.

But you must tell me the result of your experiment. It dashes my hopes of any brilliant discoveries. I much question whether, under the most favorable circumstances, you will find yourself able to satisfy yourself and others too. Those friends who love you so much will perhaps be unwilling to make demands upon you; and this will make you anxious to do all you can imagine them to desire. This is the worst of all slaveries — to be in a situation where one is not sure of all that is demanded, and where delicacy forbids the free expression of wishes. In most cases, too great requisitions are made upon the time and thoughts of a governess. There should be a rigid arrangement in regard to hours and services, leaving the time which is not employed in instruction wholly free, independent, and solitary, if desired. For a time you will be willing to give all your waking hours to your employment, and feel that you cannot do enough to serve a friend; but real teaching is an immense tax upon the mind and the health; and you have duties to yourself, the neglect of which will at last unfit you for the proper fulfilment of the very engagement you have entered into. Your own qualities of character may clash with those of the family, and you cannot be supposed to have the touchstone to their peculiarities, that members of the same family have, — an innate and fibrous knowledge, as it were, of the springs of each other's action, and the associations that govern these springs. I have never seen a more painful tyranny exercised than that over a governess in one instance; not a palpable tyranny that could be rebelled against and openly thrown off, but a total ignorance of another's wants and rights, that made the whole life a bondage. The lady who presides believes sincerely that she offers a happy home and easy duties to one whose whole time and thoughts are taxed in such a manner that she cannot feel at liberty to dispose of an hour, although many are actually left unoccupied by accident. This is an extraordinary instance of selfishness, I acknowledge, but it generally taints the relation, more or less. I have but one counsel to give to such sufferers. Sacrifice everything but independence, but preserve that inviolate; for without it one can neither be truthful nor capable of improvement. We never should allow ourselves to be in a responsible situation where we cannot express our opinions for fear of giving offence. There is enough of that servile fear in our common intercourse with our fellow-beings. Let us keep ourselves out of temptation while our daily prayer is that God may not lead us into it.

I am prepared for a theoretic refutation of all my positions, but shall probably be very self-opinionated till you have lived through this experience, as I have done.

Yours, affectionately, M.

LETTER VII.

My dear Anna, — I am somewhat reconciled to your being in a less independent situation than I wished for you, by learning that you are, after all, in a school-room of your own, surrounded by children educated thus far under various influences. The range of ages in your little company appears to me rather too unequal; but I have such confidence in your resources, that I will not forebode failure. I only hope you will not be distracted by too various calls. In my own experience, I was obliged to relinquish older and more advanced pupils in favor of younger ones, because I found the proper attention to the two classes incompatible, and in my own case my heart was with the little ones. You are better fitted to cope with older children, because your force of will is superior to mine.

I rejoice in your lovely surroundings. I once kept school near a gurgling brook, whose banks were ornamented with wild flowers, and the room was always redolent of perfumes, and garlanded with clematis and other flowers in their season. Not only children's heads, but mine, were wreathed with them; and many a lesson was given and learned under the trees, and on the grassy turf, golden with buttercups and dandelions. But now a few feet of sky, and a glimpse of verdant back-yards from one window, is all I can boast of when housed. I am blessed with the proximity of Boston Common, through which I daily wander with my little flock, and many of my children have country summers to remember, — vacations at least. Cities are unnatural places for the young. All childhood should be passed in the country, and in after-life its memories can be pitted against the evils the grown-up must bear in pursuit of certain social privileges.

I feel modest about describing my lessons, now you actually have your classes before you, and are sounding certain depths to meet the occasion. I wonder if you will begin with creation, as a friend I could name told me she did, when first meeting face to face a little disciple, her first pupil.

I am glad you do not begin with a large school. In many schools that I have visited, I have seen that the teachers were overpowered by numbers. This is apt to necessitate — no, not necessitate, for that cannot be necessary which is wrong, — but it is apt to introduce the motive of emulation, as a part of the machinery. Emulation is a passion — I call it an evil propensity, so strongly implanted in the natural constitution of man, that it needs no fostering. It should be checked and restrained like any appetite, so that its only function may be the desire to emulate noble deeds, but never to be degraded into competition for praise or honors. One of the mothers of my children thinks it is a very useful ally to induce children to study hard spelling-lessons; but I assure her it cannot be made to play into my spelling-lessons, which are natural growths out of reading-lessons. No, I banish that evil spirit from my dominions, and endeavor to teach my scholars to have a deep interest in "each other's" progress instead of wishing to rise upon the ruin of others. I have a device which answers all the purpose of a healthful stimulus, and insures some of the lawful rewards of industry.

In my present school, where the children are all under twelve, I made one class in arithmetic, including all who could count their fingers and thumbs, and, arranging them in the order of ages, began with the youngest, asking the questions in Colburn's first lessons in arithmetic, and saying that I should take the first section and let each one go through with it before I went farther. When the youngest missed a question, I marked the number of it with her name, and began at the beginning with the next in order. Some of them soon missed, others went straight through without a mistake. I simply said to the first one who did this, "You may return to your seat and occupy yourself quietly in any way you please every day at this hour until this lesson is over."

The lesson was to continue half an hour.

Those who did not go straight through, remained and took another turn after each had tried.

I had seen the pleasing effect of this mode of hearing a recitation practised upon older scholars, and knew that its charms would gradually unfold to these little ones.

The first section was accomplished by all that first day. But I gradually took longer and longer portions; and soon the pleasure of getting through, and having the disposal of little times thus gained, was very animating. I liked the effect much better than that I heard described by a distinguished German mathematician, who told me that his father, who was a soldier, had a triangle of wood made, very sharp at the edges, on which he obliged him to *kneel* while he studied his arithmetic lessons. The effect was very stimulating to his mathematical faculties, and though he hated his father at the time (a consequence I thought more of than he appeared to), he attributed to it a remarkable power, second only to Sir Isaac Newton's (who could think a train of mathematical thoughts consecutively for twenty minutes), of thinking his mathematical thoughts consecutively *fifteen* minutes.

My little people were so delighted with their leisure, thus gained, that they voluntarily studied their lessons beforehand (which I did not require), and soon I was obliged to set off the older portion into a separate class, who went on with the mental arithmetic very rapidly, while the younger ones, who recited on the same plan, and enjoyed themselves in the same way, were more deliberate. I followed the same plan with "Fowle's Geographical Questions on the Maps," which is a very nice book for children's use. It makes them very thoroughly acquainted with maps. My favorite geography lessons (and the favorite lessons of my scholars too), are oral; and I now have a course of lectures delivered on a certain day in the week by the children, which would amuse you, I am sure. I put my work-table on one end of the long writing-table, and my little lecturers stand behind it in turn, sometimes with a written lecture, sometimes with only a wand to point at maps or pictures, — and give their little lectures. One little fellow of eight would talk all the afternoon over a map if I would let him, telling stories of countries which he has heard of from me or others. Another is very fond of natural history, and her little lectures are about insects, and birds, &c. Indeed, these are their chief topics, — geography and animal life.

In arithmetic I also have many other exercises, such as arranging beans in certain numerical forms; and on the black-board I teach numeration in a simple way. I use Shaw's box of arithmetical blocks to teach the philosophy of carrying tens, and I think it admirable. I also have Holbrook's frame of balls. All these devices help to make processes clear. I find a very great difference in children in regard to arithmetic. I have had one scholar who never could go (she died at fifteen) beyond a certain section in "Colburn's Mental Arithmetic." She reached that after repeated trials; for when I found her grounded at any special point, I always turned back and let her review, and in that way she would gain a little at every repeated trial. This child found geometry easier than numbers, and mastered "Grund's Plane Geometry." She could also write out a reminiscence of Dr. Channing's sermons, or remember anything interesting in history, natural history, or anything of an ethical character. I also had one gifted little scholar who could not learn to spell accurately; but she drew with great power and beauty, — with "an eye that no teaching could give," as was said of her by a fine artist. These discrepancies in talent are very curious. Phrenological philosophy alone explains them.*

* Since these letters were written, the St. William's school established in Edinburgh by George Combe, Esq., and in which that distinguished man taught personally during the latter years of his life, has proved conclusively that the Phrenological philosophy is a fine basis for education. The principle there practised is, to cultivate assiduously those faculties which were found naturally deficient in the pupils; thus aiming to make whole men out of what otherwise would have been but fragments of men.

Having thus disposed of geography and arithmetic, in the last of which I doubt not your mathematical faculty will strike out something new, you will expect me to describe my modes of teaching language, as you know that to be my personal hobby. I think I might have other hobbies if I knew more. But I do think the teaching of language covers a great deal of ground, bringing into play, as it certainly does, so many faculties.

The first thing to be aimed at in language is, that it shall be clearly understood. It is not necessary to go out of one's own language to teach etymology. I take such words as *funny*, *kindly*, *sweetly*, and ask from what words those are derived.

"What does funny mean?" The answer will be, "Full of fun, or "Something that has fun in it." "What is kindly?" "Full of kindness." "What does agreeable mean?" "Something we like," said a little boy one day in answer to this question.

"Does every one like the same things?" said I.

"No."

"Then something may be agreeable to you that is not agreeable to me."

"Yes."

"Can you think now what the word agreeable is made from?"

He could not think.

"A thing agrees with something in me that does not agree with something in you, perhaps. I do not like the perfume of a narcissus. It does not *agree* with my sense of smell, but it agrees with some people's sense of smell."

He was pleased with this, and saw that *agree* was the word.

"From what is *lively* made?" I asked.

He hesitated.

"What does it mean?" said I.

"Oh, *lively*, why it means *very* lively!"

"Can a table be lively?"

"No, it must be something that is alive. Oh, I know now — *alive* is the word."

"What is alive made from?"

"Living," he answered.

"All these words are made from the name of something."

This brought him to the word *life*, and then he sprang up and clapped his hands and whirled round.

I do not always check these natural gymnastics.

Such lessons as these I am teased for continually. Those who have studied I can carry still farther in derivation. I sometimes reverse the process and ask for all the words that are made from *life*, *action*, &c.

Often when I give the children their slates to amuse themselves a little while, they bring me lists of words made on this principle of analysis; and I assure you that when I read to them, I am never allowed to pass by a word that is not understood. Several times when I have deliberately pronounced a very long word that I expected to be questioned upon, it has brought half a dozen of my little audience to their feet.

I was very fond, when a child, of listening to lessons upon figures of speech, given in my mother's school; and was quite expert in hunting up metaphors, tropes, hyperboles, and personifications. So I impart the same pleasure. The spiritual applications of words is pleasantly educed out of their sensuous qualities, also. "The sweet apple," and "the sweet child," are equally significant; and it is well to trace back words thus figuratively used to their original meaning in the sensuous world, for they are felt to be more significant when thus verified. It leads to sound thinking. There are so many poetical expressions in common parlance, that it is very easy to put children upon this track.

I have lately set up a little class in thinking, preliminary to giving some idea of the construction of sentences. I do not attempt to teach grammar technically to such little people as mine; but I contrive to induct it into them by certain devices, not wholly original, for they are recorded in the "Record of a School." Allow me to repeat the drilling with which I began.

I called them around me one day to have a *new lesson*, which is always joyfully acceded to by these little lovers of new things, and nothing pleases them better than to be set to thinking.

I asked them if they knew what their five senses were.

Not one had ever heard those words used together, apparently.

I enumerated; sight, hearing, smell, touch, taste.

Several individuals jumped up, whirled round, and sat down again.—

I then asked each in turn to name some object, and tell me by which of their senses they could perceive it; and by how many?

This they did readily again and again. They could see, and smell, and touch, and taste a rose, but they could not *hear* it. So of other things.

I then said, "I have a thought; do you know what it is?"

"No."

"Cannot you see, or hear, or smell, or touch, or taste my thought?"

"No."

"Now each one of you think of some object, but do not speak till I ask you for your thought."

"Can you see your thought?"

Some answered "No," others "Yes."

I asked each in turn for their thoughts. They were a bird, a house, a horse, &c., all visible objects.

I said, "All these things can be seen when they are before you; but can you see the thought?"

Some answered "Yes" to this, which I found meant that they could see the image of the thing in the mind; others said "No."

"Can you see your thinking?"

"No."

"Can you not send your thoughts out into the country, where you have sometimes taken a ride?"

"Yes."

"Can you see, smell, hear, taste, or touch your mind?"

"No."

"But is not mind a real thing? Have not you a mind that you think with?"

"Yes."

"There are some real things, then, beside those we can see, hear, smell, taste, and touch?"

"Yes."

"What other things beside your mind?"

No one answered.

"Have you any love?"

This brought many to their feet, with a shouted "Yes."

"Any happiness?"

"Yes."

"Goodness?"

"Yes."

"Naughtiness?"

"Yes."

"Is truth in the mind, or outside of it where we can see it?"

"In the mind."

I then took Mrs. Barbauld's hymns, in the first of which occur the words *reason*, *kindness*, *heart*, *life*, beside the names of many objects of the senses, and made two columns on the black-board, in which I put down respectively, as they were mentioned, all the names of objects, both of the senses and of the mind. To the latter list I added the words *God* and *soul*, by the direction of the children, upon asking them if they could think of any more such words.

I then made the same discrimination between actions of the body and actions of the mind, which they followed very well, sometimes confounding the two, as older philosophers do.

I endeavored to give them the idea that things which they see, hear, &c., exist both in the mind and out of it. This I could do by asking them if the person who made the first chair did not think of it first. Was it not in his mind before he could make it? So everything in the world existed in God's mind before he made it.

I then asked, "Which column of words gives the names of real things?"

They all said the objects of the senses were the real things.

"Can they not be broken up, or burnt, or worn out?"

"Yes."

"Can the soul, or love, or goodness, or happiness, be broken, or burnt up, or worn out?"

"No."

"Which are the things that last forever, then, — these objects of your senses, or these objects of your mind?"

"The objects of the mind."

"Does your goodness always last?"

"No."

"Where does it go to when you are not good?"

Nobody knew.

"Can you have it again when you wish to?"

"Yes."

"Who do you think keeps it for you?"

"God."

"That is what we mean when we pray to God to help us to be good."

All seemed to understand this.

"Then we find," I said, "that the real things that last forever are in the mind?"

"Yes."

"Do our bodies last forever?"

"No."

"Do we live forever?"

"Yes."

"Yes, our souls are the real things."

This was enough for one lesson. Another day I asked about the qualities of things, and added a column for such words as green, white, pretty, &c. These are the main classes, and I shall go on by degrees to words expressive of relations, and to words that are substituted for the names of persons and things which are pronouns. The children are very fond of making lists of words of this sort, and often bring them to me, divided off into their respective columns.

I have put the whole school, except the babes, into this class; and of those who know how to read well I have made a Latin class. For this I use the interlined translation of "Æsop's Fables," which Mr. G—— T—— first imported into this country. I began with a line of a fable committed to memory, with the English words beneath them. It is not only good for spelling to begin Latin early, but it gives precision to thinking, if used aright. After learning one fable, by degrees, I let the children vocabularize the words by putting the names of things into one column, the names of actions into another, as in the analysis of English; and this has given them quite a vocabulary of Latin, from which we often make lessons in derivation. Putting the nouns into a column soon showed the modifications of termination, and then I explained the difference between that language and ours in that respect, and showed them how few small words were used in Latin. They have also studied the indicative mode of the verb *amo*, and have learned to substitute other verbs in the various tenses. But I confine them at present chiefly to committing to memory the fables.

Dr. Follen thinks it well to teach German very early also, which gives the Teutonic element to our language; but I have not done this in my present school, because the difficulty of the German letter is such a puzzle to little brains.

French I only teach them colloquially as yet; for the sight of French words confuses spelling very much with little children. It is well to exercise their organs in pronouncing the words; and all my children can say many things in French.

By and by I shall show them the words, if they stay with me till they are ready for them. All these exercises of mind, if not made fatiguing by too long continuance at one time, are perennially interesting to children. The new life and vigor a little hard thinking imparts to them makes one almost a convert to a theory lately set forth by one of our contemporaries, that the scholar and thinker should be the longest lived man. I believe it will be found true, if the brain be healthily, not morbidly worked. I love to see the eye fixed in thought for a moment, even in a very young child: but I would have in the next moment a jump or a run, or a laugh; and these generally alternate with thinking, if nature is left free. I am jealous of one moment's weariness at this age. I speak particularly now of very young children, who are only too willing to think, not of the wilful, playful rogues whom it is hard to fix one moment, because they would have no work, but all play. There is a great difference, however, in children of all ages, and I would be careful of them all. Force and vigor are so essential to health of mind, as well as of body, that I would secure those first to every child.

I once had a very bright boy of four in my school, who had a very remarkable memory. He would learn a verse of poetry by my repeating it once, and learned to read with marvellous rapidity. It was almost alarming; but I took care not to stimulate him in any way. He was suddenly seized with a violent influenza, and did not return to school for two months. When he returned, he had not only forgotten all he had learned, but never showed the same aptitude again. In a year afterwards he had not caught up with those first few months. This taught me never to urge a child to exertion while suffering from a cold; and my attention having thus been directed to the point, I have often observed how that malady dulls the action of the faculties.

I have one dear little scholar now, only too willing to exert her mind; and if I see that anything seems difficult to her earnest spirit, I advise her at once to put it aside; for the tearful eyes tell me plainly that there is no need of urgency on my part, and that the danger is in too great persistence of the will for duty's sake. If it is necessary to explain the matter to others, I do not hesitate to say that that little scholar studies too hard for her health, and I do not wish her to be fatigued. It is necessary for her peace of mind to say as much as this, and the others only see more clearly what I wish them to see, that I measure them by the effort they make, not by the results they achieve. The same persistence of will and earnestness of spirit sometimes produces a violent shock of feeling in this child, if she is arrested in any of her purposes, even of play; but a gentle steadiness on my part soon brings the repentant little head on my bosom.

I often wish I knew how much moral and mental effort I ought to require of children, to keep the soul in full play and never encroach upon nature, which adjusts the balances so happily in her own way, when not constrained. I have to fall back upon my instincts for this, as the mother undoubtedly does. This adjustment has been very happily and wisely made in the case of Laura Bridgeman, one proof of which is, that an obstacle in her path is only met as a joyful occasion for some new effort. If she finds a stumbling-block in her way, instead of falling over it, or being discouraged by it, she dances round it, and apparently hails it as a new proof of the power within her to conquer all things. If her thread gets tangled when she is sewing, she laughs and adjusts it. Giant Despair would in vain tempt her, but would try again to hang himself, as when, in olden time, Truth and Holiness together escaped from his clutches. Principles, when known to her, seem to be imperative; and cut off as she is from the deceptive senses, she recognizes only the power within herself, which laughs at the defiance of insolent brute matter. It was the plan of her education that she should not be told of God's existence till she gave indication of some idea of Him; but in some way or other she became possessed of that name for the existence of absolute power and goodness (we do not know yet how far that embodiment of the idea was intuitive); and she already refers all things to His agency. One suggestion pointing towards that idea would necessarily fructify in such a mind as hers, and immediately she would have a name for the law within her which she obeys so wonderfully in conscience, and exemplifies so remarkably in her intellectual operations. She answers to me the question which I have heard asked, "Whence do the intuitions of the mind come?"

But I must go back to my little family once more. These children are quite expert printers, and have followed their fancies very much as to what they printed; as, favorite stories or scraps of poetry, for I did not wish the process to become tedious. One day I let each dictate to me a short story, which I wrote down as they dictated; and while they were full of delight I proposed that they should write stories themselves, instead of copying them. This they subsequently varied with writing what they could remember of my readings to them; so now I am overwhelmed with compositions of all sorts, and often very good ones. I have always thought it well for children to write a good deal, and I have never found any difficulty in making them like to do it. When I read or tell them anything I wish them to write, I often put leading words on the black-board, to suggest the order of the story, or the description; or, to spell difficult words. One child writes funny stories, and laughs herself as she writes; another gives descriptions of natural scenery, in the midst of which her characters find themselves. One writes about wolves and other horrors. I have a variety of pictures hanging on the walls, and I sometimes propose that they should write stories about them. These writings are all printed with lead pencil, or on the slate, because the mechanical difficulty of writing script with the pen makes it tedious to children.

I shall look impatiently for your account of your proceedings. I believe I have told you the principal things I endeavor to teach, but it is impossible to describe all the occasions on which one can minister to the inquiring minds of children. I suppose many persons would think I give too much time to playing and singing, but I do not often invite people into my school, for my ideas of order are different from the ordinary one of sitting still and not speaking. I am perfectly content as long as the lifting of my finger or the tinkling of my little bell will reduce my subjects to order.

I forgot to mention that one day in the week we resolve ourselves into a sculptor's studio. I seat the children around one of the long tables and let them model in clay. They make miniature vases, and even faces, and who knows but what some genius may be developed?* Paper cutting is also one of my arts. It teaches forms as well as drawing, and some of these children cut very decent birds and other animals. Sometimes I draw for them to cut, and I have shown them the properties of a circle by cutting one and dividing it up into angles, acute and obtuse, and teaching them to put them together again. I was much pleased myself when I first understood the relation of angles to a circle, and find that other children also enjoy it. I let them play with the Chinese puzzle also, which exercises their inventive faculties.†

If all teachers loved to play with children as well as I do,

* One of these children subsequently evinced much talent for the plastic art, which she traced back to this opportunity. She always kept it up, and gave fair promise of accomplishing something in this department of art.

† Several years after these letters were written, the Rev. Thomas Hill issued a series of cards containing geometrical figures composed of triangles of different sizes. They were very useful in aiding the development of the mathematical faculty in a private family, and might be used with advantage in the present Kindergarten-schools, whose success forever settles the question of the manner in which young children should be taught. The above letters exemplify the blind gropings of a true child-lover after that which has now been so beautifully developed by observation and genius united.

I think they would discover what I think I have; that children need superintendence in their plays to defend them against each other. The only danger is, that the older person may lead too much, and not sufficiently follow the leading of the children. When children do work at anything, they should be taught to do it accurately and well; but a concentrated effort should be very short. I hope everything, as I told you, from your discoveries in this charming science, of which I am never tired, I am never weary of talking about my little flock, and all the little flocks I have from time to time presided over. The last always seems to me the most interesting; especially the younger ones. A new little being just waking up to a consciousness of the world environing it, is a new study to me always, one of which I never tire, as I am very apt to do of older people. When you have taught a few years, we will compare notes again.

Very affectionately yours,

M.

I. Lord's Prayer.

II. The Fishes.

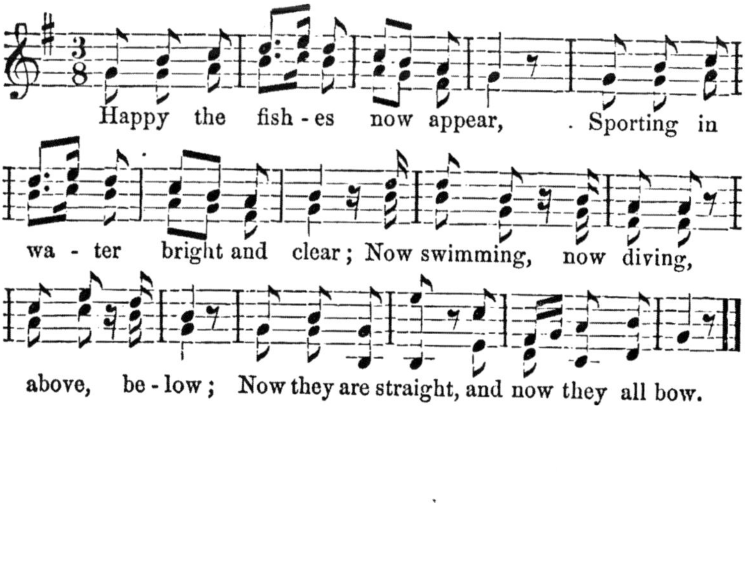

III. Brotherly Love.

2.
Angry words they never speak,
Promises they never break;
Unkind looks they never show;
Love sits smiling on each brow.
O, how lovely, &c.

3.
They are one in heart and mind;
Courteous, pitiful, and kind;
Willing others to forgive,
And make happy all who live.

4.
When at home, at school, at play,
They are cheerful, blithe, and gay;
Always trying to increase
Human pleasure, social peace.

5.
If we for each other care,
All each other's burdens bear,
Soon the human race will be
Like one happy family.
O, how lovely, &c.

IV. At the beginning and close of play, is sung:

V. The Pigeon House.

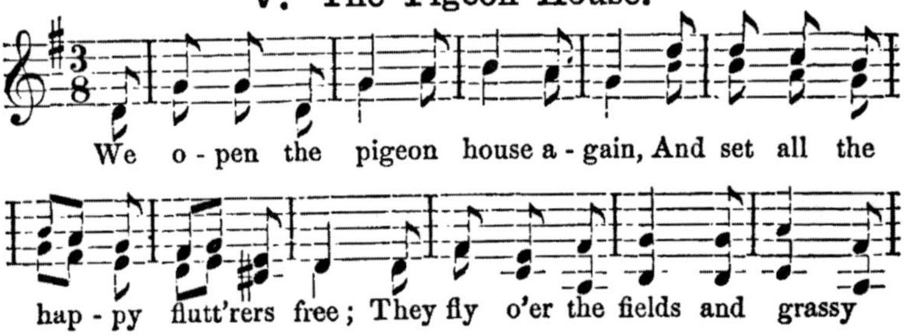

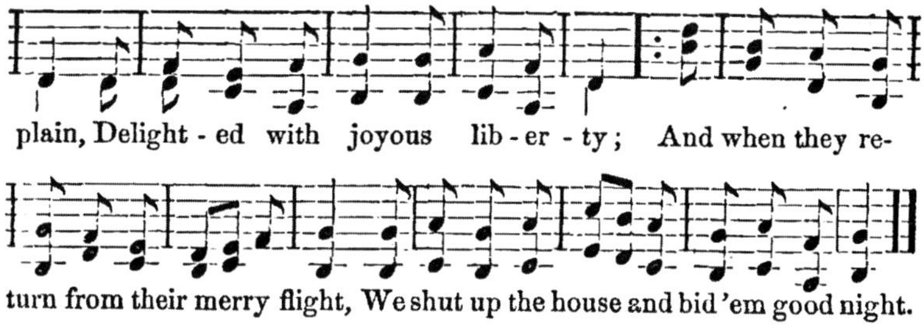

VI. The Cuckoo.

VII. The Peasant.

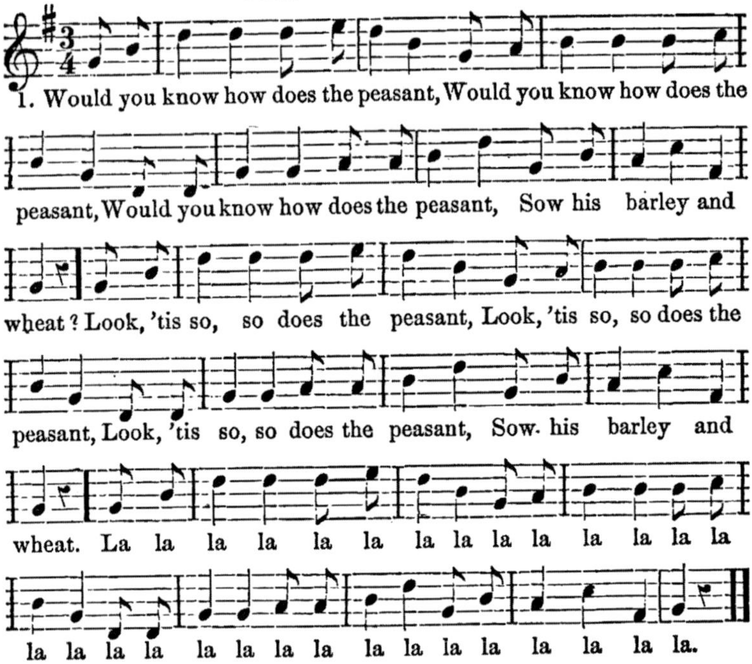

2 Would you know how does the peasant
Reap his barley and wheat?
Look, 'tis so, so does the peasant
Reap his barley and wheat. La, la, la, &c.

3 Would you know how does the peasant
Thrash his barley and wheat?
Look, 'tis so, so does the peasant
Thrash his barley and wheat. La, la, la, &c.

4 Would you know how does the peasant
Sift his barley and wheat?
Look, 'tis so, so does the peasant
Sift his barley and wheat. La, la, la, &c.

5 Would you know how rests the peasant
When his labor is done?
Look, 'tis so, so rests the peasant
When his labor is done. La, la, la, &c.

6 Would you know how plays the peasant,
When his labor is done?
Look, 'tis so, so plays the peasant,
When his labor is done. La, la, la, &c.

VIII. The Sawyer.

Let us now leave off our sawing,
Rest awhile in pretty playing,
  Playing, playing, playing so;
Playing, playing, playing, playing,
  Till 'tis time to saw again.

IX. The Cooper.

X. The Wheel-barrow.

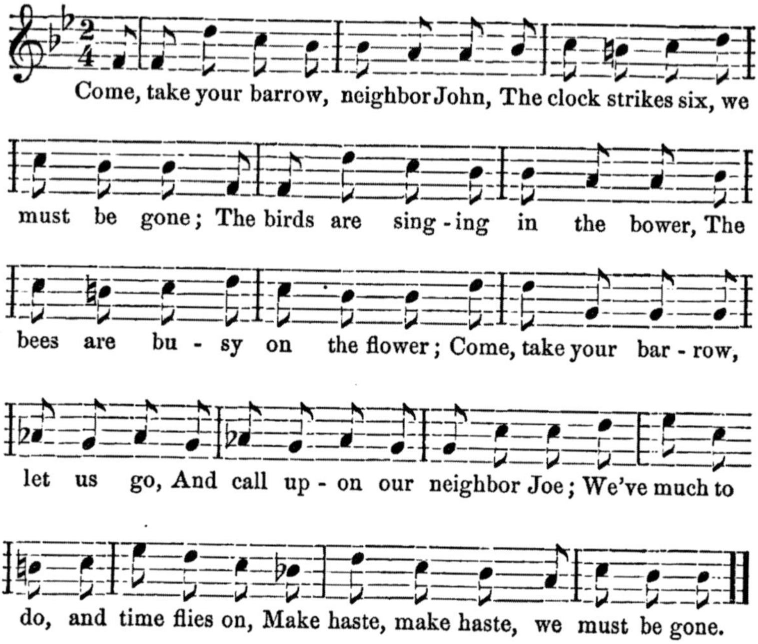

XI. The Clappers.

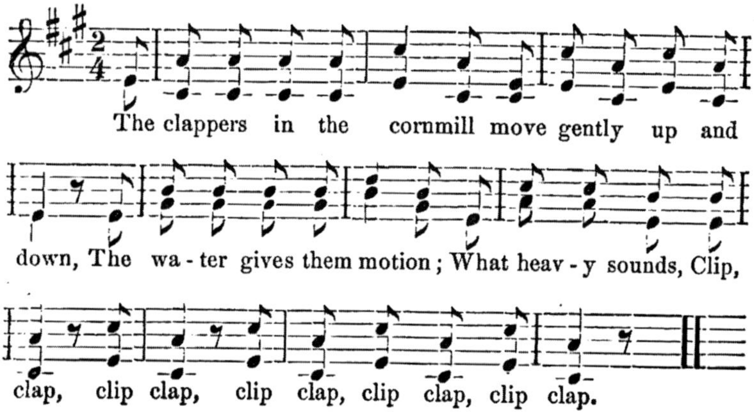

XII. & XIII. Windmill and Water-wheel.

or, XIII. See the WATER-WHEEL, how she goes,
While the water freely flows, &c.

XIV. The Pendulum.

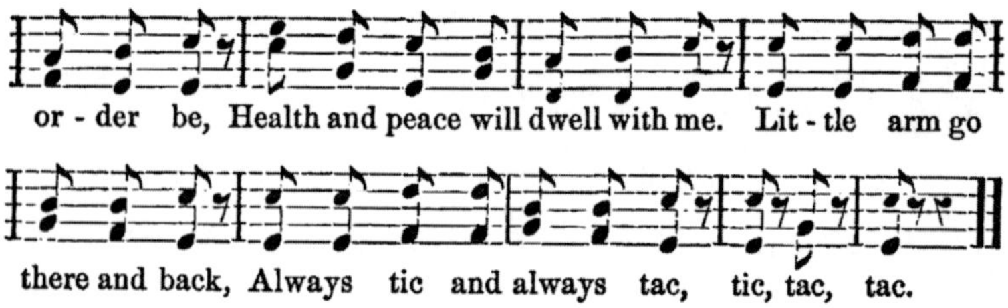

XV. The Rovers.

XVI. The Weathercock.

XVII. The Bees.

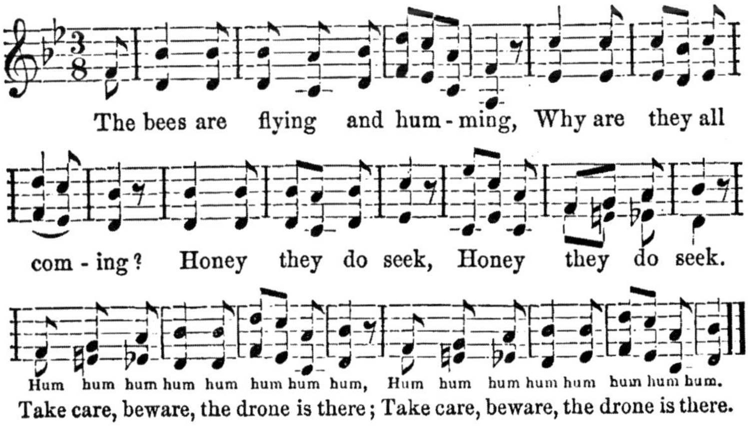